Twayne's Filmmakers Series

Warren French
EDITOR

Mizoguchi

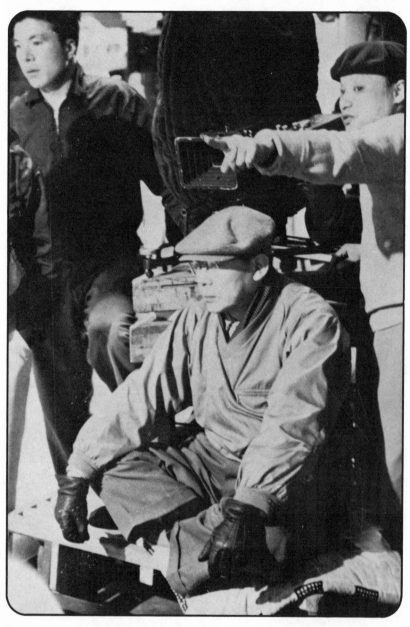

Kenji Mizoguchi (center) with director of photography Kazuo Miyagawa, shooting
Street of Shame *(1956).*

Mizoguchi

KEIKO McDONALD

University of Pittsburgh

BOSTON

Twayne Publishers

1984

Mizoguchi

is first published in 1984 by Twayne Publishers,
A Division of G. K. Hall & Company
All Rights Reserved

Copyright © 1984 by G. K. Hall & Company

Book Production by John Amburg

Printed on permanent/durable acid-free paper and bound
in the United States of America.

First Printing, May, 1984

Production Stills courtesy of the Film Library Council of Japan.

Library of Congress Cataloging in Publication Data

McDonald, Keiko I.
Mizoguchi.

(Twayne's filmmakers series)
Bibliography: p. 172
Includes Index.
1. Mizoguchi, Kenji, 1898–1956.   2. Moving-picture
plays—History and criticism.   3. Moving-picture—
Japan—History.   I. Title.
PN1998.A3M4898   1984   791.43′0233′0924   83-26507
ISBN 0-8057-9295-3

91.430233
miz
wed

Contents

About the Author

KEIKO MCDONALD was born and raised in Nara City, Japan. After receiving her college education in both Japan and the United States, she completed her Ph.D. work in English literature at the University of Oregon.

Professor McDonald has taught at the University of Oregon and the University of Texas at Austin. Currently she is an associate professor in the Department of East Asian Languages and Literatures at the University of Pittsburgh where she teaches courses in Japanese literature and cinema as well as comparative literature.

Professor McDonald's publications include a book, *Cinema East: A Critical Study of Major Japanese Films.* Her essays on Japanese film and literature have appeared in *Literature/Film Quarterly, Film Criticism, Literature East and West,* the *Japan Interpreter,* and the *Journal of the Association of Teachers of the Japanese Language.*

Editor's Foreword

OF THOSE who might be called world-class film directors, Kenji Mizoguchi enjoyed probably the shortest period of international celebrity during his lifetime. After a nearly thirty-year career, directing forty-eight silent and twenty-seven sound feature films, at the age of fifty-four Mizoguchi found himself a cinematic luminary and national treasure when *The Life of Oharu* won a Silver Lion at the Venice Film Festival. He won this coveted honor a second time the following year with perhaps his most famous film, *Ugetsu*, which received also the Italian Critics Award; and for an incredible third time in a row he won in 1954 with *Sansho the Bailiff*. But, tragically, this passionate artist mellowed into a maturity few filmmakers achieve; he had only four more years to live, during which time he completed four final films of declining power.

Even today, retrospective tributes to the work of Mizoguchi, like the one shared with the films of Ozu at the New York Film Forum in May and June 1983, concentrate upon the late films, although this program offered also *Sisters of Gion* and *Osaka Elegy* (1936) and *The Story of the Last Chrysanthemum* (1939), all of which Keiko McDonald concentrates upon in this study as among Mizoguchi's most significant early talking pictures.

The reasons for the singling out of the few relatively late films are easy to understand, since most of Mizoguchi's silent works are lost, and neither the surviving *The Song of Home* (1925) or *White Threads of the Cascade* (1933) are easily available, although both also receive detailed treatment in this book. The films of Japan's imperialistic years culminating in World War II indicate the artist's discomfort and lack of inspiration during the period (the two-part *The 47 Loyal Ronin* made during the war provides, as Keiko McDonald explains carefully, insights into the artist's problems).

Despite the greater familiarity of the late work, as this book also points out, not all film historians and critics are convinced of its superiority to

Mizoguchi's earlier work, so that some more comprehensive knowledge of this master's whole career is necessary if an international audience is to develop a balanced conception of the director's problems and achievements. As the first book-length study devoted to Mizoguchi to be published outside Tokyo, Keiko McDonald's study, which has been researched principally during visits to Japan, provides the long-needed starting point for making Mizoguchi's whole career, unified by stylistic and thematic elements that qualify him, like only a few others, for the designation *auteur*, better known and understood throughout the world.

Because of Mizoguchi's productivity and the disappearance of much of the early work, it has been regrettably necessary to limit discussion of the films not generally available. We hope, however, that this book will be followed by a more specialized study based on Professor McDonald's exhaustive study of what can be reconstructed about Mizoguchi's early years and the early Japanese cinema.

This book is, however, more than an introductory guide to Mizoguchi's work. It will especially interest those concerned with feminist studies, since Professor McDonald focuses especially on Mizoguchi's lifelong concern with his female characters, particularly with what this critic identifies in her account of *Gion Festival Music* (1953, just at the height of Mizoguchi's greatest period) as the theme of "the sacrifice of women in a money-dominated, male-oriented society," as these characters "act out the woman's choices (or nonchoice) between conformity and rebellion."

Keiko McDonald also demonstrates how, in dealing with this powerful theme, Mizoguchi himself progressed from the temperamental rebelliousness of his early days as a filmmaker to the sublimity of his trilogy which brilliantly "lifts his social concerns to a more universal plane" that accounts for the broad appeal of the work that climaxed his career.

Professor McDonald also pays special attention to the distinctive techniques that Mizoguchi developed to obtain the especially captivating pictorial effects that distinguish even some of his uneven films and that bring to his best works a flowing cinematic vision that parallels the irresistible flow of life itself as many of his notable characters are consumed by the society that they have sought to transcend.

W. F.

Preface

IN THE QUARTER century that has passed since Kenji Mizoguchi's death in 1956, he has come to be regarded as one of his country's three most distinguished directors, the others being Yasujirō Ozu and Akira Kurosawa.

Kurosawa's specialty is the dynamic exploration of universals, of political, social, and moral themes. Ozu is the poet of Japanese family life, the master of a cinematic technique as rich and evocative as it is simple and restrained.

Professional and amateur viewers alike award Mizoguchi the palm for his portrayal of women, and for his enrichment of themes related to them through a skillful balancing of traditional and experimental modes of cinematic art. He is also a celebrated stylist, a master of pictorial composition, of evocation of atmosphere, of a one-scene, one-shot method he has made peculiarly his own. Then, too, his ability to inspire actresses to surpass themselves has become a legend in the Japanese film industry.

The critic who thinks of writing a comprehensive study of such a multifaceted artist may be forgiven for thinking of the word temerity. Yet such a study is long past due, especially now that Mizoguchi's fame embraces East and West.

I owe my impulse to undertake this book to chapters on Mizoguchi in two recent books.

The first is Joan Mellen's chapter on him in *The Waves at Genji's Door: Japan Through Its Cinema* (1976). Mellen's feminist perspective unintentionally slights the subtle cultural contexts Mizoguchi's women inhabit. His films, though famously sensitive to woman's plight, cannot be reduced to formulas. No Mizoguchi film was made to state, *tout court*, that to be born a woman is to be born a slave; or that to exist as a woman is to be sacrificed. This is not to say that Mellen's critical method is faulty; merely that Mizoguchi's treatment of women must be given the benefit of the richer human and aesthetic contexts he labored to set them in.

My second impulse derives from a chapter devoted to Mizoguchi in Noël Burch's *To the Distant Observer: Form and Meaning in the Japanese Cinema* (1979). Burch brings a strictly semiotic, political approach to a dozen Mizoguchi films, and puts proper emphasis on their modes of representation as revealed in shot size, camera movement, and filmic composition. However, he is so eager to explain particular patterns of signification that he fails to show how these signifiers can be related to the contextual meanings of the film—the process of signification. Moreover, his neglect of recorded speech as an important signifier in these films is surprising.

At present, the student of Mizoguchi can turn for basic information on films and secondary sources to *Kenji Mizoguchi: A Guide to References and Resources* (1981) by Dudley Andrew and Paul Andrew. The present work is the first critical book on Mizoguchi in English. Like my first book, *Cinema East: A Critical Study of Major Japanese Films*, it seeks answers to a basic question: how can the critic born and raised in the Japanese tradition show Western viewers how to "read" Mizoguchi's films?

There are, I think, three ways to arrive at appropriate answers. The first is to study what for me is the most intriguing thing about Mizoguchi's art: the close interaction of his thematic and aesthetic aims, his perfect marriage of content and form. As another leading director Nagisa Ōshima has said, Mizoguchi thinks through his camera. I hope to show how he does this; and how his search for new subjects and modes of representation constitutes a steady progress leading over the years to a uniquely personal style and mastery of cinematic art. Representative films chosen for comment cover quite a long period, from *Furusato no Uta* (*The Song of Home*, 1925) to *Akasen Chitai* (*Street of Shame*, 1956).

Considerations of form and content also ought to illuminate Mizoguchi's famous dedication to themes connected with women. Here, my emphasis will be on Mizoguchi's progressively more universal conception of human existence. (I see this not as a feminist, but as a critic interested in contextual and aesthetic approaches.)

The second area of inquiry has to do with the man himself. Mizoguchi's biographers have always been fascinated by the striking correlation between the art and the life.[1] The film critic Hideo Tsumura considers Mizoguchi the only Japanese director capable of creating tragedy, because his life, like his art, was tragic.[2] Yoshikata Yoda, Mizoguchi's longtime and long-suffering scriptwriter, has said that "contradiction very often was the core of his life."[3]

Though many critics insist on a clear-cut division between the artist's life and his work, and thus claim for the work a kind of perfect self-consistency, I think such a distinction and claim is counterproductive here. Mizoguchi's life and work are too essentially "one" for such a separation. Contextual analyses predominate in my study, but I will also consider the autobiographical elements in various films because these offer the Western student valuable insights into the cultural milieu Mizoguchi dealt with so masterfully.

Finally, I will assess Mizoguchi's achievement as a whole. Some critics—Noël Burch, for example—locate the high point of his career in the thirties, with films such as *Gion no Shimai* (*Sisters of the Gion*, 1936) and *Zangiku Monogatari* (*The Story of the Last Chrysanthemum*, 1939). His postwar period is seen as a decline. I would argue that, on the contrary, Mizoguchi's artistic growth reaches full maturity in the fifties, with films like *Saikaku Ichidai Onna* (*The Life of Oharu*, 1952), *Ugetsu Monogatari* (*Ugetsu*, 1953), and *Chikamatsu Monogatari* (*The Crucified Lovers*, 1954).

Perhaps I should add that though this book is designed to serve a general audience, descriptive analysis has been kept to a minimum. I regret that considerations of space have forced me to omit an in-depth analysis of many fascinating and formative works from the thirties. One such was *Aienkyō* (*The Straits of Love and Hate*, 1937). This film is hard to come by even in Japan, and I hope to publish a separate monograph on it and other prewar Mizoguchi films.

KEIKO IWAI MCDONALD

University of Pittsburgh

Acknowledgments

THIS BOOK would not have been accomplished without the kind assistance of many people.

I owe my deepest debt of gratitude to Donald Richie who offered constant encouragement and spurred me on to complete this comprehensive study, always making himself available for the perusal of the individual chapters and for constructive criticism.

I particularly would like to thank Warren French for his generous and valuable suggestions.

I am also grateful to Jan-Paul Malocsay for taking so much time to scrutinize the manuscript and offer me stimulating comments from the viewpoint of the American audience.

My special thanks also goes to Tadao Satō, whose conversation provided so much insightful information on Mizoguchi's films.

I am also indebted to Dudley Andrew and Paul Andrew for generously furnishing me with an up-to-date bibliography of Mizoguchi's films.

Sadamu Maruo and Masatoshi Ōba at the Film Center of the Tokyo Museum of Modern Art were marvelously accommodating. Without their help and patience, I could not have studied Mizoguchi's films in such detail. I would also like to thank Akira Shimizu for locating stills in the collection of the Japan Film Library Council.

This study was supported through generous grants from the University of Pittsburgh, the Japan Iron and Steel Federation Endowment Fund of the University of Pittsburgh, and the University of Pittsburgh Center for the International Studies, and I thank them all.

Finally, I must pay tribute to my husband Charles, without whose day-to-day support and encouragement I might never have made it.

Chronology

1898	Kenji Mizoguchi born in Tokyo, 16 May.
1905	Enters elementary school. Father goes bankrupt. Elder sister, Suzu, adopted by a geisha house.
1911	Sent to a relative in Aomori Prefecture for apprenticeship. Completes elementary school education.
1912	Returns to Tokyo.
1913	Apprenticed to a firm which designs summer kimono patterns. Sister Suzu becomes a mistress of Count Matsudaira.
1915	Leaves father to be taken care of by his sister.
1916	Studies oil painting.
1917	Works for the advertising department of a newspaper in Kobe.
1918	Returns to Tokyo.
1920	Begins work as assistant director for the Mukōjima Studio of the Nikkatsu Company.
1923	Makes debut as director with *The Resurrection of Love*. Moves to the Taishōgun Studio of the Nikkatsu in Kyoto after the Great Earthquake.
1925	Stabbed in the back by his mistress. Removed as director for *Shining in the Red Sunset* because of the scandal.
1926	*A Paper Doll's Whisper of Spring*.
1927	Marries Chieko Tajima, a dancer.
1928	Involved in "tendency" films like *Tokyo March* and *Metropolitan Symphony*.
1930	Makes his first sound film, *Home Town*.

1931   Moves from Nikkatsu to Shinkō Kinema Co. Sent to China on location for *The Dawn of Manchuria and Mongolia*.

1933   *White Threads of the Cascade*. Moves to the Daiichi Eiga Co.

1936   Beginning of his partnership with scenarist Yoshikata Yoda in *Osaka Elegy* and *Sisters of the Gion*.

1937   *The Straits of Love and Hate*.

1939   Moves to the Shōchiku Studio in Kyoto. *The Story of the Last Chrysanthemum*.

1940   Beginning of his work with actress Kinuyo Tanaka.

1941   *The Loyal 47 Ronin: Part I*. His wife confined to a mental hospital.

1942   *The Loyal 47 Ronin: Part II*.

1943   Travels to the Continent with Yoda in preparation for a patriotic potboiler.

1946   Elected president of the Labor Union of the Shōchiku Ōfuna Studio. *The Victory of Women* and *Utamaro and His Five Women*.

1948   *Women of the Night*.

1951   Leaves the Shōchiku for the Shin Tōhō and then the Daiei Co. Beginning of his partnership with director of photography, Kazuo Miyagawa. *Miss Oyu*.

1952   *The Life of Oharu*, released by the Shin Tōhō, wins a Silver Lion at the Venice Film Festival.

1953   Another Silver Lion for *Ugetsu*. Also receives the Italian Critics Award for *Ugetsu*.

1954   Silver Lion for *Sansho the Bailiff*. *The Crucified Lovers*. Receives distinguished Art Recognition Award from the Japanese Ministry of Education.

1955   Makes *The Princess Yang Kwei-fei* as a joint venture of the Daiei Co. and the Shaw Brothers of Hong Kong. *New Tales of the Taira Clan*.

1956   *Street of Shame*. Mizoguchi dies of leukemia on 24 August in Kyoto.

1

The Formative Years of a Director (1898–1930)

Childhood and Early Life (1898–1920)

KENJI MIZOGUCHI was born on 16 May 1898 in Yushima Shinka-chō, Hongō, Tokyo—a middle-class district. A sister, Suzu, was seven years older, and a brother, Yoshio, seven years younger. Their father was a carpenter and roofer who went bankrupt when Mizoguchi himself was seven. The father sold their home and moved the family to Asakusa, the plebian downtown Tokyo area. Poverty also forced the father to put his fourteen-year-old daughter up for adoption at a geisha house and, ultimately, to send the eleven-year-old Kenji to northern Japan to live with relatives. This meant that Mizoguchi attended school for just six years—a handicap that burdened him with feelings of inferiority long after he had achieved success as a filmmaker.

In 1915 his mother died. At about this time father and son began to grow apart as brother and sister became increasingly close. After her adoption, Suzu had become a geisha "redeemed" by Count Matsudaira first to be his mistress and later his wife. Biographers of Mizoguchi see these traditional, yet painful, elements of Japanese life projected into films such as *Nihonbashi* (1929, now lost) and *Orizuru Osen (The Downfall of Osen*, 1935).

At fifteen, Mizoguchi was apprenticed to a designer of patterns for summer kimonos. After his sister became Count Matsudaira's mistress, she sent her brother to study Western painting in the studio of Kiyoteru Kuroda, who worked in the new impressionist manner.

The young art student also acquired a passion for the stage. He was a frequent visitor to the Western-style girlie shows in Asakusa and an avid fan of Japanese variety theater as well. The latter introduced him to traditional genres such as *kōdan* ("historical narrative") and *rakugo* ("comic story").

Doubtless his early training in the visual arts had much to do with the fine sense of composition that later became his trademark as a

(Top) A scene from Nihonbashi *(1929), one of Mizoguchi's lost silent films; (bottom), Ayako (Shizue Natsukawa) and Fujimura (Yoshie Fujiwara, second from right) in* Home Town *(1930), Mizoguchi's first sound film and second surviving film.*

filmmaker. But literature, along with literary genres at work in the theater, left its mark as well, for Mizoguchi was a wide-ranging and studious reader from his early years. He read Tolstoy, Zola, and Maupassant along with Japanese novelists like Sōseki, Kōyō, Kyōka, and Kafū. While Zola, Maupassant, and Kafū led him to value the methods of naturalism (especially where women from the lower classes were concerned), Tolstoy and Sōseki stimulated his awareness of life as it is contemplated by the philosopher. Similarly, Kōyō's works and the narrative *kōdan* together awakened his interest in panoramic and allegorical views of the drama of human life.

The beginnings of Mizoguchi's lifelong fascination with the sufferings of women also dates from this formative period. The melodramatic Meiji novelist Kyōka was especially important, since he depicted male-female relationships in a sentimental yet consciously aesthetic style. His theme was the female heart's devotion rewarded by unrequited love.

This tragic woman also figured importantly in the repertory of *shinpa*, a popular dramatic genre that set itself off from kabuki drama by using contemporary settings and situations. As we shall see, the influence of *shinpa* on Mizoguchi was very great indeed.

A certain defensiveness so important later in his career also dates from these early years. Like many self-made men, Mizoguchi read hard and sought out formative experiences, in a conscious attempt to achieve personal integration. Like many such men, too, his hard-won self-education made him touchy and aggressive with those whose accomplishments derived from years at school.

In 1918, Mizoguchi took a job as an advertising designer for a newspaper in Kobe. There the eyes of the naive twenty-year-old were opened to the facts of actual slum life and chronic, seemingly irremediable privation. This awakening, along with bitter childhood memories of poverty and dislocation, helped confirm him in the belief that the poor are victims of environmental forces. Many of his films reflect this view, among them his first, Ai ni Yomigaeru Hi (*The Resurrection of Love,* 1923).

Mizoguchi was not in Kobe long. Homesickness and frustration took him back to Tokyo, where he applied to his sister for help. He hated his father for sacrificing mother and sister to family claims, yet he himself fell readily into an exploitative pattern with the long-suffering Suzu. She gave him money and found him jobs which he was too restless to keep. Perhaps here, too, is an important formative element of the future filmmaker: the one who would display such sympathetic insight into woman's self-sacrifice in a world of selfish men.

Then, in 1920, after a year of doing absolutely nothing, Mizoguchi met Masashi Tomioka, a *koto* teacher. It was a fateful encounter. Tomioka knew Osamu Wakayama, a director at the Nikkatsu Studio who was persuaded to hire the twenty-one-year-old Mizoguchi as his assistant.

Early Films—Mostly Lost

Mizoguchi arrived at Nikkatsu in the nick of time. The studio was meeting competition with some challenging innovations. These included new methods of scriptwriting and techniques such as cross-cutting and the close-up.

Two major conventions of Japanese cinema stood in the way, however: female impersonators; and the *benshi*, who provided live commentary like the narrator in *bunraku* puppet theater. Nikkatsu wanted to hire some women for women's roles, but this attempt was temporarily halted by strong opposition from the still-influential female impersonators. A showdown followed, with the female impersonators going on strike and then losing out to a studio decision to fire them.

No doubt Mizoguchi benefited by this turmoil, but he must have been a speedy learner too. Just two months after he became an assistant director—and at the age of twenty-four—he made his first film, *The Resurrection of Love.*

Later on, Mizoguchi would make a name for himself as a director whose personality and artistic methods could be savagely contradictory. The germ of this tendency can be seen in his film debut. From the innovative young director/critic Norimasa Kaeriyama he adopted two novel tendencies: preference for a realistic rendition of the given subject; and letting the camera, as it were, do the talking. Thus *The Resurrection of Love* tells the story of proletarian struggle in a resolutely naturalistic fashion (which suffered somewhat from censorship). The *benshi*, too, are left out of it. Mizoguchi relied on an audacious number of subtitles to do the work of the live commentator. He did, however, honor two stage conventions still in use in Japanese cinema: the *shinpa* style of acting; and reliance on the center front shot of the actor's entire body.

This year of apprenticeship (1923) was the most prolific of Mizoguchi's life. He made nine films in genres ranging from mystery to psychological drama. Of course films were quickly made in those early days—the average shooting time in Japanese studios was a week.

September 1923 marked another turning point in Mizoguchi's life: The Great Kantō Earthquake destroyed the metropolis and the Nikkatsu Studio as well. The company then decided to regroup in a merger with its Taishōgun Studio in Kyoto. As a Tokyoite, Mizoguchi felt out of place at first in the genteel climate of the ancient capital, but he came to love its traditional atmosphere and settled there for the rest of his life.

His first film there was *Tōge no Uta* (*The Song of the Mountain Pass*, 1924), based on a play by Lady Gregory. This was followed in the next two years by no fewer than fifteen films—comedies, *shinpa* tragedies, and foreign adaptations.

For most of 1925 Mizoguchi suffered what seems a well-earned creative slump. His career also suffered from another source. While he was making *Akai Yūhi ni Terasarete* (*Shining in the Red Sunset*, 1925) he was stabbed in the back by a low-class geisha. Because of the unsavory newspaper publicity, he was replaced on the set by another director.

His reputation may have been damaged, yet it is easy enough to see in this episode a kind of formative influence, too. Later in life he would exhibit his scar and say: "You cannot portray women unless you have been stabbed like me!"

He had quarreled violently with this geisha, and directly experienced the love/hate dichotomy he would later explore in his films. Those same explorations show that he also was a sensitive observer who was aware of the pathos of a woman from the depths whose folly in love puts her even more at the mercy of hostile environmental forces.

Furusato no Uta (*The Song of Home*, 1925)

Furusato no Uta is Mizoguchi's twenty-sixth film and the earliest to survive. Though simple-minded and doctrinaire in its working out of the city versus country theme, it does show us the young director doing assigned, and doubtless not very congenial, work. His material, however, does have a certain historical interest.

The protagonist Naotarō is anxious to leave for the city and education, but poverty ties him to village life and work as a carriage driver. The aim of the film is to set him straight: he must learn to appreciate the home place and its values.

The city and its values invade the countryside in the persons of some former elementary schoolmates who bring with them the superior airs and know-how and bad manners of a city education. They disrupt village life by throwing parties and showing off, causing impressionable yokels to neglect the evening meetings of the agricultural club. The message is unmistakable: it is a far better thing you country people do, staying at home and tending your gardens (much like the message in the American D. W. Griffith's *True Heart Susie* in 1919).

As might be expected, the manners and morals of melodrama are never far away. Naotarō is visited by his former school principal and a foreign education inspector just after he has saved the inspector's daughter from drowning—and refused reward money. Learning of the boy's poverty, the inspector offers to pay for his education in Tokyo. Naotarō's reaction is presented in the simplest possible terms. First, point-of-view shots of his sister and parents show how unhappy the inspector's offer has made them. Then a medium shot of Naotarō's sober countenance is followed by the subtitle message: "I will remain in this village. To become a conscientious farmer is the most important thing in my life."

Mizoguchi's favorite motif of ambitious man helped by devoted woman finds no place in this naive piece of propaganda. No woman is instrumental in the hero's transformation. Instead, the film relies on a juxtaposition of town and country, modern and traditional values to do this work. As an evocation of Japanese village life in the 1920s, it is interesting, even (given the benefit of a past recaptured) charming.

This film also contains some memorable compositions, as at the end, when Naotarō has resolved his conflicts and become a true son of the soil. A quick montage shows sunshine breaking through clouds to brighten a field with a single scarecrow. Two shots of heads of rice plants waving in the wind end in a dissolve. Then we see Naotarō at work tilling the soil. Another dissolve yields to a horse moving across the field and that, too, yields to a shot of a family harvesting together. At this early stage of Japanese cinema, montage was frowned upon as a foreign innovation. Mizoguchi's use of it here seems fresh and sensitive, and may have been an experiment influenced by his predecessor at the studio, Minoru Murata.

In any case, by 1926 Mizoguchi pulled himself together and began to make films which bear the marks of his personal style. No print survives of *Kaminingyō Haru no Sasayaki (A Paper Doll's Whisper of Spring)*, but critics of the time praised it for the naturalistic and sensitive treatment of conflict created by male egotism and frustrated love. Along with these hallmarks of the Mizoguchi style they also noted his inspired use of setting: downtown Tokyo is captured with authority and control. He would always do best with materials he knew intimately, and throughout his career would pay a price for taking up subjects he knew at second hand.

Mizoguchi was more consistent, early and late, about using only established artists for major roles. He refused to accept new talent for these, even talent urged on him by studios as having obvious potential. Mizoguchi considered the training of his stars a burden and a limitation. Thus his reliance on strong performance can be seen in the features he turned out in 1926. These are workaday pictures, but they feature established stars. The *shinpa* drama *Shin Ono ga Tsumi (My Fault–New Version)* is one example; another example is *Kyōren no Onna Shishō (The Passion of a Woman Teacher)*, a love-triangle ghost story.

Mizoguchi followed his round half-dozen films of 1926 with two mediocre ones in 1927: *Kōon (The Imperial Grace)*, made at the request of the army; and *Jihi Shinchō (The Cuckoo)*, a melodrama based on a novel by Kan Kikuchi.

Kaneto Shindō lays the blame for such a poor showing squarely on a woman named Chieko.[1] Mizoguchi met her in 1927 at a dance hall in Osaka, was immediately infatuated, and proposed marriage. But Chieko was married already—to a *yakuza*, or gangster. Mizoguchi persisted nonetheless, and thanks to the good offices of a well-placed friend, prevailed on the lady to change her gangster for a filmmaker.

Thus at twenty-nine, Mizoguchi became the model uxorious husband of a relentless harridan. It is said that his art came to owe much to the battle of the sexes fought on the home front; and that losing consistently to Mrs. Mizoguchi at home prepared him for his day at the studio. At work, the accommodating husband became the dominating filmmaker whose specialty was male-female love-hate relationships. In this capacity he was an all-day screaming and yelling dictatorial monster who vented his fury on actors and staff, regardless of sex, persistently and implacably until he achieved precisely what he wanted.

While 1928 and 1929 were unproductive years for Mizoguchi, the Nikkatsu Company was enjoying great success with period films (*jidaigeki*) like Daisuke Itō's trilogy *Chūji Tabinikki (The Travel Diary of Chūji Kunisada)*. Mizoguchi was shocked and edified by his rival's dynamic cinematography, the rapidly rotating camera especially, but he knew better than to attempt a genre with whose materials he was not familiar.

Instead, he turned again to the world he knew so well—that of the *shinpa*-style novels of Kyōka. His film *Nihonbashi* (1929) no longer survives, yet its plot shows how close to home Mizoguchi was willing to come in his search for material. *Nihonbashi* concerns a young man's search for his elder sister, who became a geisha in order to put him through school and then vanished. In spite of the obvious parallel with his own life, Mizoguchi apparently failed to invest the human relationships in the film with any satisfactory reality, though he seems to have succeeded in creating the atmosphere of Kyōka's world.[2]

The year of the international financial crash, 1929, remained a period of routine studio assignments for Mizoguchi. *Asahi wa Kagayaki (The Morning Sun Shines)* was a promotional picture made at the request of a newspaper, the *Asahi. Tokyo Kōshinkyoku (Tokyo March)* was a box-office hit because it promoted the title hit song record![3]

In this year, too, the film industry recognized that the newly emerging proletarian literature of Japan had commercial potential. The result was a genre called *keikō eiga*, or "tendency film." Mizoguchi had been personally instructed in the anticapitalist ideology of the proletarian movement by one of its forerunners, the writer Fusao Hayashi, who stayed with the Mizoguchis for a while. *Tokai Kōkyōgaku (Metropolitan Symphony,* 1929) was Mizoguchi's only bonafide tendency film. The script was drawn from several proletarian writers, and dealt with a poor boy and girl victimized by the rich. The results were heavily censored.

By this time, Mizoguchi was preparing to make his first talking picture, *Furusato (Home Town,* 1930). Sound had been introduced to Japan as early as 1926, but got its real start in 1930, when the film and recording industries began to collaborate in earnest. Japan's first successful talkie was released in 1931: Gosho's *Madamu to Nyōbō (A Neighbor's Wife and Mine).* Before that, Mizoguchi's effort (the third talkie produced at Nikkatsu) would appear and suffer from serious technical flaws.

Furusato (Home Town, 1930)

This second surviving Mizoguchi film is important since it marks his first attempt to work in a medium that would free him from a stylistic constraint: the subtitle frames of the silent screen. As one critic notes, he differed from directors like Yasujirō Shimazu, Yasujirō Ozu, and Heinosuke Gosho from the Shōchiku Kamata Studio in his choice of the sequence, not the single shot, as the basic unit of his films.[4] Subtitles interrupted flow, and as Mizoguchi's subsequent development would show, flow was to be the *sine qua non* of his best work.

Oddly enough, *Home Town* was a popular film in spite of technical flaws which touched the essence of a plot that deals with a singer's career. The voice in this case belonged to Yoshie Fujiwara, a tenor whose enormous popularity may have been the drawing card.

In most respects, the film is melodrama as usual: the story of a woman's unselfish devotion to a talented egotist. The action is organized in four contrasting movements. In the first, the impoverished tenor Fujimura struggles into the limelight, aided every step of the way by Ayako. The second movement provides the contrasting marital crisis. Fujimura, spoiled by success, indulges in a life of luxury under the influence of his female patron, Natsue. Ayako leaves him. A career contrast takes over in the third movement. Fujimura is injured; he may never sing again. In the fourth movement the balance is restored. Ayako and Fujimura are reunited, evil is put to flight, and he resumes his career, a new man.

Each sequence in this film is filled with information organized for effective visual and acoustic contrast, especially since Mizoguchi experiments with a wide range of Western cinematic devices—dollying, close-ups, montage, tilting, etc. At the same time, we see the beginnings of his preference for a characteristically Japanese mode of presentation: the long take.

Despite some effective scenes along the way, the ending of the film reveals its essential mediocrity. The characteristic tunefulness of early talkies everywhere is there, along with a famous tenor to back it up with the best of his popular repertoire (title song included). His profile is too often, and insipidly, followed by a close-up of Ayako's happy face. Even some "tendency film" ideology puts in an appearance, as Fujimura sermonizes on the notion that art belongs to the proletariat.

With the Manchurian Incident of 1931, Japan entered into an imperialist phase that would have momentous consequences for the film industry. Nineteen thirty and thirty-one were not productive years for Mizoguchi. Besides *Home Town*, he made just two films, both undistinguished: *Tōjin Okichi (Mistress of a Foreigner*, 1930) and *Shikamo Karera wa Yuku (And Yet They Go*, 1931). The former is interesting, however, since it shows how early Mizoguchi took up the one-scene, one-shot method he would develop so beautifully later on.[5]

2

The Struggle to Break with Tradition
(1931–35)

Departure from Nikkatsu

ABOUT THE time Mizoguchi completed *Shikamo Karera wa Yuku* (*And Yet They Go,* 1931), a radical change took place at the Nikkatsu Studio. The new management began to dictate to directors who had enjoyed a fair amount of independence before. As a result, Mizoguchi left for another Kyoto company, Shinkō Kinema, after he made *Toki no Ujigami* (*The Man of the Moment,* 1932).

His first project at Shinkō was *Manmō Kenkoku no Reimei* (*The Dawn of Manchuria and Mongolia,* 1932). This propaganda film about the Manchurian Incident (which marked the beginning of Japanese imperialist expansion) was a complete failure. Mizoguchi's shooting was so haphazard that no amount of editing could give shape to the finished product.[1] In fact, Mizoguchi abandoned the project before it *was* finished, and refused to undertake any further work for six months.

However, in 1933 he emerged triumphant with *Taki no Shiraito* (*White Threads of the Cascade*) which *Kinema Junpō,* the leading journal of that period, called the second best film of the year.

At this time, too, Mizoguchi's famous "diabolic" tendencies surfaced. Shigeto Miki, his cameraman for *White Threads of the Cascade,* had this to say: "He was a demon when he worked on the film. . . . He caused a lot of trouble for those who worked for him. He would always remind them of how great he was. . . . He would never compromise. . . . And so he was the kind of person whose compromises could not be relied upon. . . ."[2]

Taki no Shiraito (*White Threads of the Cascade,* 1933)

White Threads of the Cascade, a silent film, was Mizoguchi's second attempt at a Kyōka novel, the first having been the undistinguished

27

Nihonbashi (1929). As before, the subject matter is melodramatic. The heroine Shiraito is a circus performer who falls in love with a poor student Kinya. She works to send him to law school and eventually is brought to trial for murder. The prosecutor appointed to her case is Kinya. The film ends with the suicides of the lovers.[3]

In this film Mizoguchi succeeds in transforming Meiji-period melodrama into powerful drama on a subject familiar in his work: suffering humanity embodied in a woman. His achievement here is largely attributable to a more mature handling of the cinematic devices which would also become familiar hallmarks of his style: long takes and dollying. Even more important are several exquisitely composed single shots, for these redeem a work rather unjustly neglected.

The opening sequence anticipates a style of continuity later put to good use in films like *Sisters of the Gion* and *Ugetsu*. The dollying, tilting camera executes a carefully controlled shift from general to particular. First we see the circus tent. Then the camera dollies diagonally along the audience inside. Thus we identify with the packed house and excited mood of anticipation among the spectators. A quick cut to a banner tells us what we need to know: it announces the *Taki no Shiraito Troupe*. "White Threads of the Cascade," the literal translation of the leader's name, also refers to her famous "art of water" act so popular in summer. This in itself conveys a sensory impression and adds to our shared sense of anticipation of her appearance. Yet Mizoguchi makes us wait. After a subtitle announcement that spectators come only to see Shiraito and her famous show, he prolongs our suspense by cutting first to the audience, then panning toward the stage curtain.

Clearly, the buildup of our curiosity relies on the sequential rhythmic continuity of the camera work: it continues. A long shot of the stage with the spectators in front of it suggests that the act is about to begin. Yet it does not. Instead, we are given two shots, close-ups of a drum, then a *samisen*. Why does Mizoguchi abandon his notable preference for sequential movement for these abrupt cuts to stage props? He is even on record as being opposed to such things:

> Directors often show a close-up of a small wind chime. The poetic atmosphere emerging from the chime swinging in the air or things like that should not be presented in such a manner. A prop in close-up is unnecessary except when its detailed part is related to the context of the drama. I hate close-ups.[4]

The exception at hand does serve the context of the drama—thematically and rhetorically. The drum and the *samisen* accompany Shiraito's act. Our impatience as members of the audience is checked; as viewers, sure enough, we are taken backstage in a shot which reveals Shiraito and her friends getting ready to perform.

Perhaps the most memorable moment in the film comes in the scene depicting Shiraito's second encounter with the obscure young man she has fallen in love with. The scene opens with some conventional business showing Shiraito walking across a bridge and discovering a young man sleeping there. A close-up of her face registers surprise and joy, yet no corresponding close-up of the sleeping figure tells us why. Instead, we see Shiraito in a long shot putting her shawl over him; then the camera tracks up to reveal the sleeping Kinya. There follows a rather abrupt transition as the camera switches to a low-angle shot from the level of the bridge; then, as the camera holds steady, the rhythmic variation of the shot is created by the verticals of the composition. The actress Takako Irie is an unusually tall and slender woman, so her standing figure takes on a specially exquisite character as her beauty blends with the atmosphere created by the summer night and the young man sleeping at her feet. Clearly the camera eye invites us to share the director's gaze of admiration.

Though Mizoguchi would become remarkably chary of close-ups after 1936, he uses them freely in this film, and with notable ingenuity, especially in respect to timing. This is particularly evident in a scene depicting Shiraito's musings in a train as the troupe travels through the countryside. By this time, a series of intercutting between Kinya in Tokyo and Shiraito on tour has established the conventional wisdom according to which city life means bad influences and country life good. Thus life in Tokyo is making the passive Kinya more insensitive to Shiraito's devotion, while contact with rural life is expressive of her pure feminine dedication to the man she loves.

Rural scenery also serves as a seasonal indicator of the fortunes of a troupe like Shiraito's. Her "art of water" is much less of an attraction in fall and winter, so her livelihood, like the farmer's, is tied to nature. These facts are conveyed in a cut from the train running along under the clear autumn sky to a tree shown in close-up. A pan down among the leaves reminds us of leaves falling. Similarly, our sense of Shiraito's worried sense of financial hardship (in supporting Kinya's studies) is given final form by another close-up from nature: the chestnuts in her lap.

Though there is no explicit *boudoir* scene in this film, it does contain subtle and powerful elements of eroticism. Mizoguchi handles these in a manner characteristically Japanese. Thus he ends the encounter on the bridge with a sudden break in the compositional flow, cutting from the lovers in a sitting position to Shiraito's naked feet in *geta* ("wooden clogs"), in close-up, of course. This evocation of feminine sensuality is similar in effect to the woodblock prints of Utamaro's women. Here, the shot is used to depict Kinya's first awakening to Shiraito's physical charms.

The scenario for *White Threads of the Cascade* was particularly troublesome. Mizoguchi put the original writer to work on a great many revisions, yet remained unsatisfied. Two more writers were called in with the same result, so that in desperation Mizoguchi began shooting without a complete script. Thus the film was made by increments, on a day-to-day basis subject to change on the spot—changes this director did not hesitate to make, much to the consternation of his actors. Even so, *White Threads of the Cascade* offers a preview of mastery to come, and remains a film whose fine moments more than make up for its serious flaws.

Mizoguchi's next film, *Gion Matsuri (Gion Festival*, 1933), was another studio assignment. This adaptation of a *shinpa* play of the same title focuses on a daughter's sacrifice of herself to family interests and her subsequent unfulfilled love. This ready-made Mizoguchi material yielded a mediocre film, largely because of undue haste in shooting— three weeks.

Switching Companies

Gion Festival was followed by a political film *Jinpūren (Jinpū Group*, 1934). Though interested in politics, Mizoguchi never succeeded with highly charged political subjects. Thus this film about a samurai revolt in the Meiji era proved to be a disappointment.

Dissatisfied, Mizoguchi left Shinkō Kinema in 1934 to work for Nikkatsu once again—this time at their Tamagawa Studio near Tokyo. He stayed just long enough to make one film, *Aizō Tōge, (The Mountain Pass of Love and Hate*, 1934). The print has not survived. The plot concerned a melodramatic love affair between a Liberal Party supporter and an actress. According to Shindō, the result was "an old-fashioned film reflected Mizoguchi's preference for the Meiji era in a negative way."[5] Yet apparently it also provides evidence that the prototypical Mizoguchi heroine—the dedicated, long-suffering woman—was well established by this time.

Still restive and dissatisfied, Mizoguchi left Nikkatsu for another company, the Daiichi Eiga. Though he stayed with them for only two years, he did work that turned out to be important for his artistic development. The company in this case must be given some credit, since its flexible production policy left directors free to choose their own subjects. For Mizoguchi, this would mean freedom to create such masterpieces as *Osaka Elegy* (1936) and *Sisters of the Gion* (1936).

Mizoguchi also made three others films in those two years. *Orizuru Osen (The Downfall of Osen*, 1935) was his third adaptation of a Kyōka novel (after *Nihonbashi* and *White Threads of the Cascade*), but it was poorly received in spite of its innovative cinematic techniques. Then he tried to break with the Meiji literary tradition, the romantic world of Kyōka especially, by turning to Maupassant's "Boule de Suif" which he adapted for *Maria no Oyuki (Oyuki the Madonna,* 1935). This too was a commercial and artistic failure. He then returned to the Meiji era for *Gubijinsō (Poppy,* 1935), based on a novel of the same title by Sōseki. Again, he failed. Despite more interesting camera work, critics tended to see only evidence of his inability to cope with the intellectual world of a Meiji literary giant. It was true that Mizoguchi had no idea how to portray an intellectual woman, a creature foreign to his experience.

In any case, this series of failures threw him into a deep depression which he suffered till *Osaka Elegy* appeared in 1936 and success brought new energy and better spirits.

Orizuru Osen (The Downfall of Osen, 1935)

This important transitional film sheds a somewhat different light on Mizoguchi's sustained thematic interest in female self-sacrifice within the Meiji literary tradition. The heroines of his previous adaptations of Kyōka novels paid dearly for their heroism. In *Nihonbashi,* the sister disappears for the sake of the brother she loves. In *White Threads of the Cascade,* the young man's benefactress and lover ends as a suicide. The heroine Osen suffers even more melodramatically en route to destruction.

Osen comes upon Sōkichi, a poverty-stricken young ricksha driver who is attempting suicide. Though she is virtually the slave of con men, she dissuades him from killing himself. She dedicates herself to helping him, but, unfortunately, her efforts result in his being drawn into the underworld with her. Eventually, they escape. She hopes to put him through medical school. Unbeknown to Sōkichi, her efforts are less successful than they seem. Having pawned all her possessions, she is forced to take up prostitution. Then, though she is innocent of any crime, she is dragged off to jail and subsequently vanishes. She regrets having "failed" Sōkichi, yet he eventually becomes a doctor. Having lost sight of Osen, he returns home from abroad and finds her wandering insane (from syphilis) in a crowded railway station. He attempts to cure her, but it is too late. She dies raving mad with the light of a terrible false happiness in her eyes.

While the plot itself suggests the limitations of this film, it is nevertheless interesting for two reasons. First, it gives evidence of Mizoguchi's increasingly avid interest in formal experiment with the camera. And second, it offers some beautifully memorable moments, scenes whose dramatic intensity derive from Mizoguchi's treatment of the given subject matter.

The opening sequence is boldly complex: two sets of flashbacks are vivified by smooth panning back and forth. The first is a flashback within a flashback: the doctor, Sōkichi Hata, recalls his boyhood, and that boy (in the doctor's recollection) recalls his earliest memories. The second flashback is Osen's memory of rescuing Sōkichi from suicide. Abrupt transitions from present to past, and vice versa, provide a fresh, modern quality to this sequence, especially since the movement back and forth enhances each character's keen awareness of the impact of the past upon his life—as if the past influenced the present in some fatalistic way.

One memorable dramatic scene depicts Osen being dragged away by the police. Sōkichi comes in as she is being led away, her hands tied with rope. A close-up shows her saying: "Sōkichi, please forgive me." Then, in a medium shot of them both, she faces the camera to say: "Sōchan, I have already prepared your breakfast." A shot of Osen crossing the bridge yields to a shot of Sōkichi in pursuit. After more cross-cutting between the two (in close-up) we see Osen blowing something to him. Another long shot of her being taken away interrupts, as does another medium shot of him in pursuit; then he is knocked down by a ricksha and the camera travels to show us that Osen has blown Sōkichi a paper crane—that romantic make-a-wish image whose poignancy the Japanese audience instantly understands in this situation. No particular stylistic dexterity is displayed here; only close-ups controlling audience perspective. Yet the scene provides a powerful emotional uplift by using the most ordinary, even banal, means for suggesting the "sublime" character of this woman's sacrifice. The paper crane clearly expresses Osen's heartfelt hopes for Sōkichi's success—and a corresponding lack of concern about her own fate.

This film also provides a number of interesting uses of close-up, which at this period Mizoguchi still uses freely. One of the most interesting serves a definite rhetorical purpose. We are shown the deranged Osen's face close-up in the railway station, because the surrounding crowd no longer exists for her. Her point of reference is fixed on the memory of her happy days of altruistic sacrifice. The pathos of her plight is all the more moving since she is not aware of it herself. However, this is not the moment for easy identification with Osen. Instead, Mizoguchi invites a troubled contemplation of her derangement; we "connect" with Osen's fate only by understanding the place of such a woman in the scheme of things, that is, in this particular social context. It is precisely the averted, vacant quality of her gaze in this close-up that commands our full attention to all that lies behind it.

Maria no Oyuki (Oyuki the Madonna, 1935)

After its release, the critic Tadahisa Murakami had this to say about *Oyuki the Madonna*:

*Oyuki (Isuzu Yamada) ready to offer herself to the army officer
she later comes to love in* Oyuki the Madonna.

[It] is a better film than *The Downfall of Osen.* The first half especially reveals Mizoguchi's cinematic gifts as he presents the passengers in a carriage, each with an uncertain future. The second half, however, is more like a whimsical experiment, as is shown in Mizoguchi's treatment of the heroine.[6]

Many critics nowadays would disagree, seeing *Oyuki the Madonna* rather as a step in the wrong direction, a film made in haste and with little enthusiasm. (Mizoguchi was in fact pressed for money at the time.) The camera work is undistinguished, and the transposition of social milieu from the France of the Franco-Prussian War to Meiji Japan (during the Seinan War) seems to set obstacles in the way of Mizoguchi's usual expertise with studies of female character.

Even so, there are indications that Mizoguchi had something interesting in mind. His mannered approach here seems intended as a search for a new dimension for the thematic pattern established in his earlier films: feminine sensibility unrewarded.

This is evident in his use of Maupassant's original. Whereas the French writer intended to satirize the bourgeoisie in a panoramic view of personal and class relations, Mizoguchi concentrates on the figures in the foreground: for the facts of his two women's lives define them as society's victims. In place of Maupassant's single despised woman, Boule de Suif, Mizoguchi uses two lower-class prostitutes. By mixing these unfortunates with persons of a self-consciously higher class, he shows how the despised prostitutes are the victims of merciless avarice, ambition, and compromise.

Moreover, his two women exhibit lively instincts for survival that derive from opposing orientations. Okin is for resistance, for meeting hostility with all the small hostility someone in her position can display. Oyuki, however, stands for acceptance, for submission to circumstance. Though a social outcast herself, she is still capable of compassion.

Unfortunately, Mizoguchi's intentions are more interesting than his use of them in this film. The two women's differences remain schematic and their characters unrealized. The other passengers, too, remain stock characters, mere ineffective counters for a social satire that never takes on life.

Another fault is clearly symptomatic: elements of melodrama throughout show how hard it was for Mizoguchi to break with the *shinpa* stage tradition. This is especially damaging in the final scene, where all potential for genuine pathos is lost to melodramatic posturing, cloying music, mediocre composition, and insipid camera work. One may be grateful that Mizoguchi did so much better for female losers elsewhere in his work!

Gubijinsō (Poppy, 1935)

Yet again, Mizoguchi returned to the subject of women seen in the context of the Meiji literary tradition. And yet again, critics agree that he failed to come to grips with the world of Sōseki with its heavy overtones of intellectual skepticism about the moral issues of good and evil. Taken on its own merits, however, *Poppy* is far from a negligible piece. It marks two important stages in the development of Mizoguchi's filmmaking: his growing interest in working with contrasting female characters; and his willingness to experiment with elements of style.

Like its parent novel, *Poppy* explores the moral conflict between *giri* ("social obligation") and *ninjō* ("personal feelings") which confronts the ambitious young man Ono. He is the orphaned protégé of Tomotaka Inoue, a high school teacher. Impressed by Ono's intelligence, Inoue puts him through high school and hopes that his daughter, Sayoko, will marry him. After graduation, Ono goes to Tokyo to complete his doctorate. There he becomes the English tutor of Fujio, an upper-class woman. Inoue and Sayoko soon come to Tokyo as Ono's dependents. The rest of the plot concerns the young man's moral quandary as he is torn between the two women. If Ono is to bow to the demands of *giri*, which he owes to Inoue, he must marry Sayoko. If he follows *ninjō*, he will pursue Fujio.[7]

The conflict of values is intensified by the contrasting female characters. Fujio is the intelligent, yet calculating daughter of a rich family. A Tokyoite, she is modern in many respects: she plays the piano and studies English. She is arrogant, demanding, and downright bossy. On the other hand, Sayoko is a traditional type: an innocent, dutiful daughter. A Kyotoite, she is well versed in the *koto*, the Japanese harp. She is passive, subservient, and entirely self-effacing—so much so that she cannot expresss her feelings for Ono.

In order to emphasize the striking contrast between Fujio and Sayoko, Mizoguchi employs specific images in scenes where each woman is seen with Ono. These images contrast knowledge and experience with innocence and naiveté. Fujio's image is a gold watch. When she and Ono are first shown together in her living room, Mizoguchi cuts to a close-up of the gold watch hanging on the chest of her late father in a portrait. Fujio manipulates her suitors—Ono and her fiancé, Munechika. She bluntly asks Ono whether he wants to have the memento. The implication is clear; the one who earns her affection will be given the watch, the index of status as head of the family, the man thought worthy of managing Fujio's life.[8]

Similarly, Sayoko's world is presented through the images associated with betrothal. A picture of a bride in the traditional kimono is in the showcase of the photographer near Sayoko's house. Both Ono and Sayoko pass the shop frequently. Importantly, Mizoguchi never presents the two looking at the picture together, because he wants to show their different responses to it. Sayoko stops by the shop window and gazes at it smilingly, seeing herself in the portrait of the bride. On the other hand, Ono passes by it quickly, as if the picture reminded him of his obligation to marry her.

As circumstances combine to force a decision on Ono, we notice how freely Mizoguchi makes use of Western cinematic modes like the point-of-reference shot. Used along with other Western cinematic modes such as close-ups and reverse-field shots, and in company with the characteristically Japanese long take, the point-of-reference shot intensifies the drama and offers greater flexibility of perspective.[9] Thus the contrasting value systems represented by Sayoko and Fujio are seen as they appear to characters we can identify as morally sound in their judgments.

Mizoguchi may not have found intellectual heroines especially congenial, but he knew how to dramatize the downfall of one like Fujio. After we have seen views of her blandishing Ono—intercut with views of his intermediary telling Inoue of Ono's decision not to marry Sayoko— we feel competent to judge the entire situation. Even so, we are not surprised when Ono does the right thing, bowing to *giri*, after all. What is surprising is the extent of Mizoguchi's experimenting with Western devices like montage and close-ups in the final scene. Ono is present only in the gold watch which his rival, Munechika, is returning on his behalf. Fujio then gives it to Munechika as a token of her acceptance of his suit. To her astonishment, Munechika throws the watch into the sea. Mizoguchi catches the clash of Fujio's pride and dismay with close-ups between her face and the sinking watch. A montage of the ocean follows, indicating how the watch gradually disappears into the water. So much for a powerful atypical Mizoguchi heroine who has dared to manipulate men.

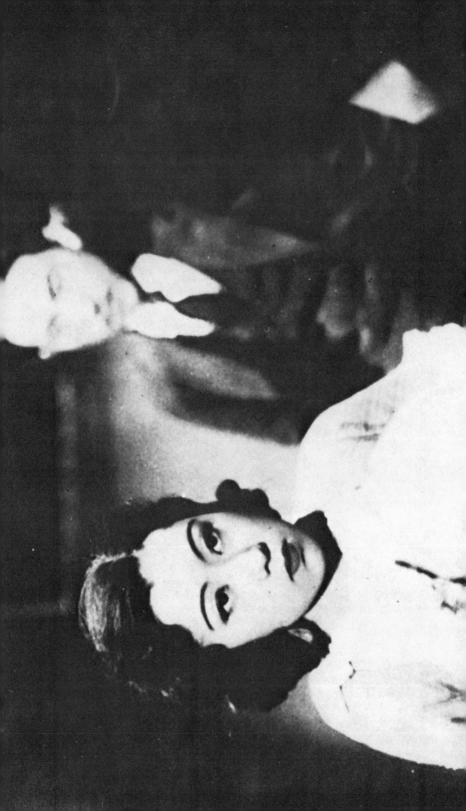

3

A Victory for Realism:
A Trilogy Minus One (1936)

Mizoguchi: Perfectionist and Tyrant

AN OPPORTUNITY to free himself from Meiji literary tradition came with *Osaka Elegy* (1936), Mizoguchi's fifty-sixth film and one which most critics consider the forerunner of realism in Japanese cinema. For the first time, Mizoguchi's eyes were open to the possibilities of his new environment, since the townspeople of the Kansai area were different in character and temperament from the Tokyoites he knew so well.

It was in this film, too, that he first worked with Yoshikata Yoda, the native of Kyoto who became his scriptwriter and lifelong friend. Unlike his contemporary Ozu, Mizoguchi hardly wrote any screenplays himself, but he was keenly aware of their importance. In fact, around this time he became an unremitting perfectionist in the matter of script. Despite a serious case of tuberculosis, the long-suffering Yoda was forced to revise the script for *Osaka Elegy* more than ten times before Mizoguchi accepted it—reluctantly. He kept telling his scriptwriter: "You must give us people so real that the audience can smell their body odor."

Naniwa Erejī (Osaka Elegy, 1936)

The "realism" of *Osaka Elegy* is difficult to define.[1] Perhaps Mizoguchi does it best himself: "Both *Osaka Elegy* and *Sisters of the Gion* portray the manners of city people in the Kansai area. I brought to these films the things I had observed in the streets and showed them as they were: the vulgar as the vulgar."[2] Certainly he points up two aspects essential to his realism: subject matter and method of presentation.

The subject matter of *Osaka Elegy* has much to do with the reality of the place. The Japanese audience spontaneously associates Osaka with a city of calculating, profit-minded merchants. When Ayako's boss and his business associates try to buy her affection outright, they are expressing

Osaka Elegy (1936): Ayako questioned by a police officer after she has taken money from Fujino.

39

the money values of the city well enough. The Japanese have always considered filthy lucre to be just that: something uncouth to talk about, much less to be flaunted. Osaka merchants, however, are seen as a self-consciously proud exception to this cultural attitude. Mizoguchi described their defiant vulgarity: "People from Osaka do not care what others think. They are too busy pursuing self-interest, too shameless to value self-restraint. . . . *Ninjō* ["humane feelings"] to them means little or nothing—and nothing when weighed in the balance against business interests."[3]

One of Japan's oldest cities, Osaka (the Naniwa of ancient times) is depicted in this film as a place where the male and his double standard reign supreme. Businessmen like Asai and Fujino can have their mistresses and enjoy them as status symbols. Respectability and license work hand in glove. Thus the doctor, Yokoo, encourages Asai to take a mistress. Infidelity should embarrass no man.

The respect accorded to money makes even a female double standard possible. Asai's rich wife Sumiko provides the contrast with Ayako here. Heiress to a wealthy merchant, she can afford a sexual freedom denied a poor woman like Ayako. No one, not even her husband, dares reproach Sumiko for deviating from the traditional female role.

In the films of Ozu, the family serves as a bulwark against the harsh realities of society at large. In *Osaka Elegy,* as in other Mizoguchi films, the family is a microcosm of society itself. Here, too, the dominance of males is a force destructive to women. Ayako's father and elder brother are too weak or too selfish to rescue the family from poverty. Instead, they take Ayako's sacrifice of herself for granted, then ostracize her for conduct that reflects on the respectability of the family. These men represent a type we see becoming more consistently defined in Mizoguchi's later films: the man whose ambition is validated through female sacrifice. Ayako's father and brother, moreover, represent an advance in egoism and callousness over their predecessors. At least Kinya (in *White Threads of the Cascade,* 1933) and Sōkichi (in *The Downfall of Osen,* 1935) come to appreciate the devotion of their benefactresses. Such a psychological transformation is not accessible to the men in Ayako's life.

Osaka Elegy explores the four basic choices of action available to this unfortunate woman, who works as a telephone operator in a small company owned by Asai and his wife. Ayako's troubles begin when her father embezzles money from his employer and cannot pay it back. Her first choice is to conform, to be the dutiful daughter in a respectable way. She tries this by seeking a loan from her fiancé.

Her second choice is compromise. In the fiercely competitive society of the early 1930s, not yet recovered from the depression, money is held dear and virtue cheap. Thus Ayako becomes the mistress of her employer, Asai. It is a case of having to do the wrong thing for the right reason. Yet this, too, fails. Her motive may be honorable, but society remains intolerant of the poor young woman's breach of conduct.

A third choice is exploitation. She must try to capitalize on her charms by taking money from Asai's associate Fujino—without risking her "chastity." This too ends badly. He has her arrested, and she is cast off by the family she sought to rescue.

A brief closing sequence depicts the final choice: rebellion. The young woman is cornered and forced to challenge openly the values of both society and family.

Each stage of Ayako's conflict is enriched by Mizoguchi's controlled camera work and attention to nuances of dialogue. Filmic texture here is to a great extent created by the Osaka dialect, which Mizoguchi took great pains to let express the character of the place.[4] In this, he had the help of veteran actors, such as Benkei Shiganoya (Asai) and Eitaro Shindo (Fujino), whose delivery embodies all the oily cunning and tenacity of Osaka's merchants and their city.

The opening sequence of *Osaka Elegy* offers an insight into Mizoguchi's use of the camera. This montage of nighttime Osaka—the flashy neon signs advertising merchandise and entertainment—is calculated to signify the Osakan's zest for profit and pleasure. Nocturnal atmosphere also furnishes a thematic link for Ayako's evolving range of choices. Forced to make use of her charms, she does so at night in a riverside restaurant. Again, at the climax of the film, when she vows to become financially independent, she is seen on a bridge at night.

The texture of the entire film, in fact, may be called nocturnal. One Japanese critic has called *Osaka Elegy* a film with "a steady gaze."[5] Mizoguchi, in fact, considered darker textures generally more effective in sustaining audience concentration on the action in a film, because they better create a sense of close-framing than open-framing.

This principle is also utilized in the confined surroundings where most of the action takes place. At work as a telephone operator, Ayako is seen in a glass booth; and as Asai's mistress, through windowpanes. This close-framing keeps the viewer intellectually involved yet emotionally detached. Similarly, the sparing use of close-ups prevents the viewer from delving too deeply into the feelings of characters. Then, too, a certain feeling of claustrophobia is entirely appropriate in a film about a young woman in fatally constrained circumstances.

After the opening night view, we greet the day in Osaka—escorted by the camera down the long narrow corridor of a traditional merchant's house. Obviously, this is the house of a man who has done well for himself—a fact that has much to do with the thematic conflict in this film.

The camera stops on Asai, who has just awakened. This true vulgarian worshipper of Mammon claps his hands and prays: "May my business prosper!"

Camera movement is restricted now. Asai sits at breakfast and expresses unhappiness with his domestic situation. Movement in this close-frame is provided by the maids going in and out. A cut takes us to a contrasting scene: Asai's wife is still comfortably asleep, her pet dog by her pillow.

A similar pattern of contrast controls the scene in which Ayako makes her first choice: asking her fiancé for a loan. Once again, Mizoguchi's concern with movement/stillness and evocation of mood asserts itself. The camera tracks and stops along with the couple as they walk at dusk near the misty waterfront. The long shot favored here creates a typical Mizoguchi mood which Donald Richie defines as resulting from the fusion of the individual characters with their surroundings.[6] Here, the gloomy mood corresponds to the hopelessness of Ayako's predicament.

Her emotional tension is explored further in a claustrophobic family scene. After she has negotiated with her father's creditors (while he peers out of hiding), she confronts family poverty at the meager evening meal. The camera rests slightly higher than the eye level of a person sitting on the floor, so the emphasis on room partitions and the unshaded lamp hanging low from the ceiling further enhances the feeling of poverty closing in. This is in marked contrast to the easeful luxury of the Asai household. There we have seen husband and wife squabble about matters smoothed over by money—which in Ayako's house is literally the root of all evil.

Another contrast of location comes with Ayako's second choice: Asai has set her up as his mistress in a fashionable apartment building. Again, the camera makes the most of the symptomatic architecture, in this case with pans and tracking shots up and down long flights of stairs. Clad now in Western dress, now in a kimono, Ayako is shown sitting in chairs, which of course are foreign to the traditional Japanese house.

Individual characters are also decentralized here, a device which Noël Burch identifies as basic "diegetic" pattern in earlier films such as *White Threads of the Cascade* and *The Downfall of Osen*.[7] Thus Ayako sits either at the far right or far left of the screen, shot from a low angle. The thematic function is to create a spatial flow associated with Ayako's temporary sense of freedom. She has made a bad bargain of it, however, as Mizoguchi reminds us. Throughout this sequence, he frequently cuts to her standing by the window, so that we see her through the panes. This is a clear reference to her continued confinement in a male-oriented society. At the same time, it provides the distance needed for Mizoguchi's realism of "a steady gaze" or intellectual fixation.

Ayako's security as a kept woman vanishes when Sumiko discovers her husband ill in bed in the apartment. Thus Ayako must make her third choice: using her charms to outwit men. A stylized opening shot introduces us to the nighttime atmosphere of a river restaurant. Most of the screen is occupied by the surface of the water, reflecting neon signs. The brightly lit restaurant occupies a portion in the upper right corner, looming up from darkness. Our attention is naturally focused on the glass window of the restaurant behind which two tiny figures move about. We can barely identify them as man and woman. Mizoguchi cuts to the interior of the restaurant. Ayako is here to meet Fujino; but she has no intention of giving Fujino what *he* wants. She calls in a geisha and walks out, taking the furious man's money with her.

The clash with her family prepares the way for Ayako's final choice: rebellion. This climactic scene consists of the following shots: (1) long shot of Ayako walking through the street screen right; (2) long shot of an empty bridge in moonlight, the moon reflecting in the water; (3) extreme long shot of Ayako standing near an electric light pole on the bridge with her back toward the camera; (4) medium shot of her from the waist up; she takes something from her pocket and tosses it into the water; (5) medium shot of her former patron's business card floating among the debris in the river; (6) medium shot of Ayako in profile; (7) medium shot of the water; (8) another medium profile shot; (9) medium shot of Ayako resting her elbow on the balustrade; the doctor, Yokoo, enters from (the viewer's) right; he stops midway, talks to Ayako, then exits left, leaving her alone on the bridge; the camera is stationary; violin music plays softly on the sound track; (10) medium shot to close-up of Ayako in profile as she walks along the bridge screen right; (11) extreme frontal close-up of the determined, even provocative, look on her face as she approaches the camera.

Mizoguchi condenses so much into this final nocturnal scene. Shot 1 arouses our curiosity about Ayako's destination. Together with shot 2, it recalls the formal composition of the opening shot of the film, and the restaurant scene at midpoint. Once more, the low-key photography holds our intellectual attention. As Ayako's figure is subsumed into the foggy night of Osaka in shot 3, the composition reminds us of her subservient relationship with her environment. The business card she tosses away signifies her rejection of Osaka's corrupt society. Here Mizoguchi poses an interesting question: As long as Ayako lives in a male-oriented society, can she escape becoming a part of it?

In shot 9, Ayako asks the doctor: "What can you do for a woman who has become delinquent like me?" Unlike Kurosawa's doctors like "Red Beard" or Dr. Sanada, who try to cure moral as well as physical diseases, Mizoguchi's Dr. Yokoo answers: "I don't know. I only cure disease, not delinquency." The doctor stands for a society which condemns woman for breaking with convention, but does not care to consider the cause of her downfall.

The final dramatic close-up shot of Ayako's defiant expression speaks clearly enough for her ultimate decision to challenge society. Yet several Japanese critics questioned the effectiveness of so abrupt an ending. They did so at a round-table discussion held just a year after *Osaka Elegy* was released. Mizoguchi was there and was suitably apologetic.[8] At this remove, no apology seems necessary: certainly the director waited while Ayako made her enforced choices; then he chose this climatic moment to explode. All through the film we, the viewers, have been carefully distanced while Ayako has been confined in one set of circumstances after another, hawked about like merchandise, then cast adrift by the society whose norms she failed to conform to, for reasons of poverty. Her location on the bridge at the end of the film clearly signifies a contrasting intention to break loose—just as crossing to the other side suggests a degree of hope.

Now, in this last shot, her defiant close-up implicates us in her decision. We are torn between conflicting claims of feeling and intellect. She has our sympathy. We want her to make a new life. At the same time, her need to do so compromises us—are we perhaps part of the structure that crushed her in the first place?

This thought leads to a measure of doubt (can she possibly make it?), and that to an appreciation of the irony of the final shot: we know more about prewar Japanese society than a young, disadvantaged, delinquent girl like Ayako is equipped to know. We see her failure written large— her fate, which will be to sell herself in order to survive at all. Even then, we see her being reduced to the human debris she has hated all along and rejects at the end of the film.

In this, we see the outraged cry of the director himself, the surge of pent-up emotion. In fact, we begin to wonder just whose personality lies behind that final close-up.

Yoshikata Yoda has something relevant to say about his director's intensity:

> He [Mizoguchi] does not have the courage to face persons, things and ideas that assail him. . . . He is timid. He is too honest. . . . He gets angry at himself. The anger and resentment which he cannot deal with makes him cry hysterically. This is the source of that intensity revealed in *Osaka Elegy* and *Sisters of the Gion*.[9]

The final close-up of *Osaka Elegy* does not reveal the feminist Mizoguchi's criticism of male-dominated society; rather it reflects the apex of his creative passion throughout the film. Into this shocking final image Mizoguchi finally distills the tragedy of one woman of Osaka who stands for many in the city—and throughout Japan.

Spurred on by feelings of professional rivalry, and heartened by the congenial subject matter of *Osaka Elegy*, Mizoguchi decided to make another film set in the Kansai area, this time in the Gion district, the traditional geisha quarter of Kyoto. As a frequent visitor to such "pleasure quarters" himself, he was confident that he could capture the essence of the place as no one else could.

Again, he chose Yoda for his scenarist. Their efforts together were rewarded once again. In competition with films such as Teinosuke Kinugasa's *Yukinojō Henge (Actor's Revenge)* and Yasujirō Ozu's *Hitori Musuko (Only Son)*, Mizoguchi's *Sisters of the Gion* was named best picture of the year by the prestigious film journal *Kinema Junpō*, with *Osaka Elegy* ranking third.

Gion no Shimai (Sisters of the Gion, 1936)

In "Tsuchi no Nioi" (The Smell of the Earth), Mizoguchi says quite plainly that his intention in *Sisters of the Gion* was to portray "the uncouthness of Kyotoites."[10] This is perhaps the core of Mizoguchi's realism. His intention is realized through his exploration of the central subject: the geisha's confrontation with a male-dominated, money-oriented society.

Needless to say, Mizoguchi's various modes of representation, especially controlled camera distance, make this thematic concentration possible. They are used to move the audience to intellectual concentration or intellectual scrutiny. Mizoguchi also takes special care to let the Kyoto dialect illustrate the dual aspect of the geisha's life: courtesy mixed with audacity, or "elegant uncouthness."

In *Osaka Elegy*, Mizoguchi dramatized a single heroine's choice of action in adapting to a similar world of materialism dominated by the male. In *Sisters of the Gion*, he takes a new approach to a similar conflict through the creation of two character types. The elder sister, Umekichi is a traditional variety of geisha, one who adheres to *giri*, understood as loyalty to her ex-patron. Her younger sister, Omocha, is a more modern type: one who exploits men for money. Omocha has a high school education, a rare asset in her profession, and despises all that the Gion district stands for. Significantly, while the heroine of *Osaka Elegy* shifts ground in her execution of values, each sister here is inflexible; each follows her own value system throughout and faces the futility of it in the end.

Undoubtedly, the extreme polarity of the sisters' orientation to their environment imposes a "neutral" point of view on the spectator. As if he were reluctant to side with either, Mizoguchi keeps the two value systems in tension, sometimes letting them clash, sometimes showing them in parallel. This is seen even in his spatial alignment of the two sisters: he intercuts between the two, shooting them now on different locations, now together.

The society faced by the two sisters is even more restrictive than that confronted by Ayako. The Gion, a licensed pleasure quarter since feudal times, has the force of tradition behind it. The geisha owes a twofold *giri*: to the proprietress who calls for her services at the tea house; and to the customer who patronizes her there. Moreover, the Gion is divided into a superior section A and inferior section B. Umekichi and Omocha inhabit the latter, less privileged and more versatile area where the geisha's duties commonly combine theatrical and sexual entertainment. Thus the two sisters are shackled to the two "arts of pleasing," each compromised by the other.

The opening sequence presents the donnée of the film: a struggle for survival in a world where everything has its price. Stylistically it offers a fine example of Mizoguchi's long-dolly technique, much more artistically controlled than in his earlier films. It begins with a lateral dolly shot through what appears to be a merchant's house. The camera moves past a large room where an auction is going on. It travels on across another room crowded with creditors, and glides by yet another where items are being sorted for an auction.

Immediately, this camera work piques our curiosity: we want to know what kind of merchant has gone bankrupt, and all the more so, since the single traveling shot has exposed us to the extent of his wealth. As in *Osaka Elegy,* Mizoguchi takes full advantage of the typical architecture of a merchant's house in the Kansai area: narrow in front and deep in back. The scene finally dissolves into what appears to be an annex at the end of a long corridor.

Mizoguchi is now ready to reveal the merchant's identity. Umekichi's ex-patron, Furusawa, a cotton wholesaler, is shown together with his wife, and his manager Sadakichi. All look sad. The rooms, empty of furniture, are in strong contrast with those presented earlier. The barking vioices of the auctioneers (on the sound track) connect this obvious misery with its source. Husband and wife must leave their house and return to their hometown.

Refusing to accompany his nagging wife, Furusawa comes to stay with the two sisters (Umekichi and Omocha). By doing so, he extends the theme of instability and conflict to another area of confrontation with the Kansai value system.

Here we are introduced to an important controlling image in this film. We see it right after Furusawa leaves his house. The scene cuts to a small alley where the sisters live. Mizoguchi is meticulous in presenting this alley. We see a long shot of Furusawa walking down it; he moves toward the camera, then diagonally across the screen from left to right. A reverse-field shot shows him walking straight away from the camera. These shots emphasize the long narrow dimensions of this cheerless sunless place. Mizoguchi's camera returns to it repeatedly, as when Omocha steps out of the alley, wearing a fashionable dress, after she has become the mistress of a wealthy merchant. Similarly, Kimura, a sales clerk, is shown waiting in the dark alley while his master goes inside the house to collect money from Omocha, only to be trapped by her charms. Thus it is clear that thematically the alley serves as prelude to each new stage of the sisters' moral conflict.

Mizoguchi uses long shots exclusively for showing people going in and out of this alley. He wants to call our attention to the environment in which the sisters live. Far from being secure and snug, the alley is damp and shadowy. Omocha and Umekichi, struggling for survival, live as if cut off from all promise of hope.

In his previous film, *Osaka Elegy*, Mizoguchi used nocturnal scenes not only to let the audience feel in tune with the heroine's environment, but also to establish the "intellectual gaze" as a basic rhetorical stance. He uses the alley in a similar fashion. He keeps coming back to it in order to make sure that the audience connects with this dark environment, sensing in it a felt reality of the sisters' world. But at the same time, suggestions of claustrophobia (caused by the closed framing) stimulate intellectual reflection—a necessary condition for appreciating Mizoguchi's realism.

Significantly, the closed frame becomes a pervasive mechanism for dramatizing the sisters' moral dilemma. For example, immediately after Furusawa walks down the alley, we see him together with Umekichi and Omocha inside their tiny house there.

As soon as Furusawa goes back out again, the sisters air their different views of the situation. Umekichi sees her duty clearly: *giri* requires that she allow her former patron Furusawa to move in with them until he finds his feet again. Omocha makes her position equally clear: Umekichi is a target larger than Furusawa. She attacks all the patrons of the Gion: "Who makes playthings of us? Men. Men are our enemies—hateful enemies. They deserve bad treatment."

Umekichi cannot agree. In a later scene, set in the ironically pleasant, sunlit precincts of a nearby shrine, the two sisters state their positions with thematic finality. Umekichi says that society has its rules and one must obey them. Omocha replies with a harsh indictment of all such rules.

From this point on, Mizoguchi keeps the divison between the two sisters' values conspicuously in view. Money, of course, serves as a convenient reference point as the sisters move steadily apart, each according to her standard of values.

Umekichi, distressed by Omocha's increasingly money-hungry scheming, leaves the house to join Furusawa who is boarding elsewhere. Omocha's determination to capitalize on her charms leads to disaster. Kimura, one of the men she has hoodwinked, kidnaps her. As they speed away in his accomplice's car, Mizoguchi makes effective use of the close-up, a device otherwise rarely employed in this film. In this instance, the close-up invites, not easy identification with the characters, but a rather more clinical view of the conflict between a furious man bent on revenge and the defiantly terrified woman who has betrayed him.

Omocha is pushed from the speeding car and seriously injured. The subsequent hospital scene brings the sisters together in a carefully dramatized study of the elder sister's devotion to the younger. A slow tracking shot involves us intellectually in each stage of Umekichi's emotional state. We see her enter the hospital corridor; the camera pans in to follow her to the door of the operating room. She stops center screen, as does the camera, as Omocha is carried out and to the left by a nurse. The camera follows the party as they head for a ward. Although Umekichi is out of frame, the tracking shot reminds us that she is moving along behind.

Once more, the sisters clash on matters of principle. Omocha's fierce denunciation strikes home this time: "I won't be defeated by men. Kimura did this cruel thing. I'll make him pay." Still, Umekichi insists that one must be sensitive to human feelings.

Omocha disappears behind a lattice screen, still abusing men. The camera holds still, focusing on the screen for a long time; finally Umekichi puts motion in the picture by walking round in front of the lattice. Thus this screen provides a stasis almost as strong as Ozu's famous vase in *Banshun (Late Spring)*. Though it lacks the transcendent presence of that vase, this screen still invites reflection on the matter at hand. We begin to ponder the impersonal nature of a universe in which women meet their fate.

The final sequence resolves the sisters' conflict in a typically ironic world view. Mizoguchi has used the image of the alleyway to suggest it all along: neither sister will escape this cramped and sunless way of life. The geisha's world is so constituted that none of her decisions or desires will alter it—or bring subservience a just reward.

At the conclusion of *Osaka Elegy*, Mizoguchi let the camera speak for the heroine's final challenge to society. Here, camera movement is kept to a minimum while the challenge is made in plain words.

Using the one-scene, one-shot approach, Mizoguchi shows us Omocha in bed with Umekichi sitting alongside. This view, together with closed framing, fixes our attention on the sisters' predicament. Omocha says: "Cover me with the quilt, sister." These few simple words, like the expressive monosyllables of Ozu's characters, say much more than any elaborate technical device ever could. We understand instantly that these sisters face the world together after all; and that this solidarity is all they have in the seamy, uncertain corner of the universe they inhabit.

Umekichi tells Omocha how shabbily Furusawa has treated her, leaving without so much as a word of thanks.[11] However, she still maintains that to have done what society expects of her is some consolation. Omocha, in a voice filled with resentment, says that after all, a geisha is a mere plaything of men. (Omocha in fact means "toy" in Japanese.) The camera gradually tracks up to her, but stops in a medium shot of her face as she cries out bitterly: "I hate men. Why does the profession of the geisha exist?"

Mizoguchi avoids ending this film with a close-up, as he did in *Osaka Elegy*, yet Omocha's cry is just as provocative and troubling as Ayako's final gaze (in close-up). Both devices challenge the entire world—ours included. Dudley Andrew has noted that "Mizoguchi was obsessed with the gait of women, with their swoons, with their averted or penetrating gaze."[12] The same obsessive energy seeks an outlet in Omocha's cry.

Even so, we feel something problematic in this ending, a hint of discrepancy between the semantic and cinematic functions here. On the surface, Omocha's cry is desperate enough to make us feel spontaneously for both these afflicted women. But the camera's position seems to urge a larger synthesis on us. We seek for a larger meaning. Thus our rhetorical stance is neutralized. Our ambivalence suggests that Mizoguchi himself was afraid to take a firmly objective view of the sisters' plight. Otherwise, we think, surely he would have fastened on it more deliberately in the end.

Trilogy Incomplete

The success of his first two films set in the Kansai area inspired Mizoguchi to round his triumph out with a trilogy. He wanted his third film to be set in the exotic Kansai city of Kobe. Suitable subject matter, however, proved hard to find. The theme he had in mind concerned the domestic life of a Japanese man married to a foreigner, yet (according to Yoda) the Tanizaki novel which inspired this idea also discouraged Mizoguchi, who found the novelist's exoticism uncongenial. He could foresee problems with creating convincing personalities for the husband and wife.

His waning enthusiasm prepared the way for a company suggestion—an idea with more universal appeal: the career of a girl who rose from servant to star performer in a touring company. Mizoguchi never got the chance to test his interest in this film, because the Daiichi Eiga Company was breaking up in 1937. Yet again, he was being forced to shift ground.

4

Mizoguchi Rediscovering: The World of Kabuki Actors and Puppeteers (1937–40)

AFTER THE closing of the Daiichi Eiga Company in 1937, Mizoguchi moved to Shinkō Kinema, an independent outgrowth of the Shōchiku Film Company, one of the giants of the industry.

By this time, Mizoguchi had learned—from his experiences with *Poppy* and *Oyuki the Madonna* (both 1935)—to be wary of transposing literary works directly into cinema. Thus, when his first assignment with Shinkō proved to be an adaptation of Tolstoy's *Resurrection*—to be released as *Aienkyō* (*The Straits of Love and Hate*, 1937)—he was determined to assimilate the original so completely that the audience would not even recognize its influence. Keenly aware of the scriptwriter's part in this, he signed on his old classmate Matsutarō Kawaguchi. They had collaborated once before, on *The Mountain Pass of Love and Hate* (1934).

The Straits of Love and Hate was also a test case for Mizoguchi's leadership in acting. Viewing this film, one is immediately struck by the astonishing development in the acting of Fumiko Yamaji in the role of the heroine; indeed, the actress seen in the second half seems to bear little resemblance to the one who plays in the first. Film legend has it that Mizoguchi rehearsed one scene with her nearly seven hundred times in three days.

Aienkyō (The Straits of Love and Hate, 1937)

"The *shinpa* tragedy, one can say, makes a grand display of the ego or will of a woman who endures her fate in tears."[1] *The Straits of Love and Hate*, Mizoguchi's fifty-ninth film, still shows the influence of his devotion to the *shinpa* tradition. In previous films like *The Downfall of Osen* and *White Threads of the Cascade*, both *shinpa* tragedies, heroines ended in madness or suicide. This time, however, Mizoguchi gives us a tragic woman in a somewhat different mold: she is endowed with a fund

53

op) Kenkichi (Masao Shimizu) begs Ofumi (Fumiko Yamaji) to
me back to him in The Straits of Love and Hate *(1937);*
kunosuke (Shōtarō Hanayagi) tends the dying Otoku
akuko Mori) in The Story of the Last Chrysanthemum
939).

of willpower which enables her to resist a callous and hostile world and even achieve a kind of happiness in the end.

As in the earlier films, Mizoguchi takes for his central problem a woman's need to adapt herself to a hostile environment. Specifically, the film asks: how is the maid Ofumi, herself illegitimate, to survive when she is seduced and made pregnant by the son of her employer? Her troubles begin in the remote alpine countryside of Shinshū (now in Nagano Prefecture) where she works as a maid in an inn. Kenkichi, the innkeeper's only son, seduces and makes her pregnant. This means she must elope with him to Tokyo. There he soon abandons her in order to return to his family. Ofumi works odd jobs to support her newborn child, then joins a troupe of traveling players. Eventually, their circuit takes her and the child back to Shinshū and Kenkichi.

The family reunion is only a brief dream. Rejected by Kenkichi's parents, Ofumi takes up with Yoshitarō, her comic skit partner who really cares for her.

Clearly, the country in this film is associated with prejudice, conventionality, and complacency. All these are embodied in Kenkichi's parents. They despise Ofumi because of her lowly origins: she is a servant born out of wedlock to a traveling entertainer. Her marriage to their son can only bring shame and disgrace to the family.

Similarly, Tokyo is associated with exploitation. There, Ofumi is cheated of what little she earns. She is even forced to put her newborn baby in a foster home. There, too, she is victimized. The woman who serves as Ofumi's intermediary pockets most of the money intended for the child.

The worst of both town and country values is represented by Kenkichi. Having taken advantage of Ofumi, who supports him while he loafs in Tokyo, he reverts to type the minute hardship arrives. When his father offers to take him back, Kenkichi deserts Ofumi and his child without a second thought.

The values which work best for Ofumi, then, are not tied to any place. The complacent, conservative "family" ethic is not a supportive value system, and will not help her to survive. Betrayed by it, she turns to its antithesis: the hand-to-mouth existence of the strolling players who offer her protection and companionship beyond the pale of social convention. In the end, she even finds a husband among their number. Until this happens, Ofumi must keep rejecting town and country values. By doing so, she turns each stage of rejection into a source of inner strength.

Mizoguchi registers some interesting changes in style to match his interest in this different sort of tragic heroine. For example, at the beginning of the film we see Kenkichi waiting for Ofumi by the back door of the inn. A long shot emphasizes the beauty of the snow-covered

Japanese Alps in the distance. Kenkichi has quarreled with his parents about his plans to return to Tokyo. His years at the university have made the family business seem impossibly remote and dull. Ofumi appears and pleads with him to take her away, now that she is pregnant.

All this occurs while the camera's position is fixed in a series of long shots, all but one taken from a consistently high angle. Surprisingly, the close-up is not important in this scene. In films like *Sisters of the Gion* and *Osaka Elegy,* Mizoguchi had used close-ups to invite intellectual scrutiny, and in some cases, empathy. Here, he seems to prefer watching his heroine from a distance. The pictorial beauty of the composition is undeniably present; but we are shown the lovers blending in with the wintery landscape from a distance. No rhetorical ambiguity comes into the emotional interaction here. We have, instead, a long-shot focusing our interest on conflicting value systems as a desperate, strong-willed woman urges a weak-willed, selfish man to do the right thing.

Mizoguchi uses another version of this distancing system at the finale. Here, the camera backs away from the stage to place us among the actual audience of a comic skit performed by Ofumi and Yoshitarō. Clearly, we are invited to contemplate the rewards of Ofumi's learning process. Betrayed by both town and country, she has nevertheless managed to rebuild her life. This heroine ends as mother, wife, and performer. Mere independence is not the ultimate value index here, as it was for Ayako at the end of *Osaka Elegy.* Ofumi's values are not tied to any locality, but they are tied to family. Even her independence as a performer requires partnership with her husband.

Likewise, it is no accident that this film ends with husband and wife performing a comic skit: this transposition of harsh reality into farce is a way of making the world meet them on their own terms. This kind of transcendence was scarcely available to Mizoguchi's earlier man and woman.

This period also marks the beginnings of what co-workers considered Mizoguchi's obsessive perfectionism in acting. Performers were baffled and angered by this:

> What teaching he did was very general: he told them that they were headed for a certain destination. He would not say exactly how they were to get there. The performers had to figure some things out for themselves—to live and create themselves. Mizoguchi thought that this involvement in the joy of creation built confidence. . . .[2]

The political climate from 1937 on was anything but favorable to the film industry. The prevailing militarism led to heavy government censorship and, by 1940, to rationing of film and technical materials. Worse

yet, directors were required to make patriotic potboilers like Mizoguchi's second project at Shinkō Kinema, *Roei no Uta (The Song of the
Camp*, 1938). This film, like others of its kind, was designed to
popularize its title song, and like all of Mizoguchi's potboilers, was a
commercial failure. He was, in fact, so disgusted with himself for even
making such a film that he almost quit his new company.

In any case, he directed his last film with Shinkō Kinema six months
later: *Aa, Kokyō (Ah, My Home Town*, 1938). In this picture, Mizoguchi
sought to depict a woman's challenge to the pressures and changes of
values created by big industry moving into a small town. The film is now
lost, but according to critics of the time, it failed to get beyond a
melodrama of commonplaces, despite some memorable local scenes
captured in superb photography. Again, this failure was attributed to
Mizoguchi's lack of enthusiasm for the project.

The beginning of 1939 found him still depressed. Always one for quick
action, he decided to leave Shinkō Kinema for the Shōchiku Ōfuna
Studio. This move was to benefit his career greatly, since it gave him an
opportunity to contemplate an ambitious trilogy: *Zangiku Monogatari
(The Story of the Last Chrysanthemum*, 1939), *Naniwa Onna (The
Woman of Osaka*, 1940), and *Geidō Ichidai Otoko (The Life of an Actor*,
1941).

Some credit for this success must also be given to the production
policies of the Shōchiku Company. Two years before Mizoguchi's arrival,
it had lost a superstar, Chōjirō Hayashi (now Kazuo Hasegawa), to the
rival Tōhō Company. The Shōchiku management decided to cope with
this serious blow to box office receipts by reviving an old specialty:
melodramas featuring heroines. These were a potential box office draw
for a huge female audience. Since Mizoguchi's forte had always been his
sensitive portrayal of women, he felt confident of success in this genre.

As it happened, a *shinpa* play, *The Story of the Last Chrysanthemum*,
was enjoying a sensational stage success when Mizoguchi came to
Shōchiku. He immediately set about planning a film version. His un-
bounded enthusiasm for this project was evident from the outset. He
took special pains with casting the lead roles. He insisted that no one but
the famed kabuki actor Shōtarō Hanayagi could play the hero.
Mizoguchi had decided to use the one-scene, one-shot method consistently throughout, in order to give a kind of rhythmic intensity to the
film. To realize this cubic concept, he needed an actor capable of giving a
sustained performance. Hanayagi, a seasoned stage performer, was an
inspired choice; but he was already forty. The question was: could the
veteran kabuki actor, adept as he was at makeup, play a twenty-year-old
hero?

The solution to this difficulty came in the form of a technical inspiration: Mizoguchi decided to rely on the long-shot taken through a wide-

angle lens. He also felt that this combination would be a significant innovation in filmmaking technique. As we shall see, this almost accidental solution to a problem helped change the very foundations of Mizoguchi's art.

Casting the heroine was not so easy. The first choice actress was subjected—like the staff—to three days of the worst perfectionist harassment the always tyrannical Mizoguchi was capable of delivering. She was then dismissed and Kakuko Mori brought in to take her place.

Zangiku Monogatari (The Story of the Last Chrysanthemum, 1939)

"The *shinpa* tragedy, one can say, makes a grand display of the ego or will of a woman who endures her fate in tears."[3] Tadao Sato's definition bears repeating because it speaks so well for Mizoguchi's intentions in this adaptation of *shinpa* to film. Otoku, the heroine of *The Story of the Last Chrysanthemum,* does endure a cruel fate, but she is no passive sufferer. She has the courage of her convictions, and finds self-fulfillment through independent action. Thus Mizoguchi combines in her the outstanding qualities of three of his recent heroines: like Shiraito in *White Threads of the Cascade,* she is a devoted sister-mother; like Ofumi in *The Straits of Love and Hate,* she is a faithful wife; and like Omiyo in *Oh, My Home Town,* she is a rebel activist.

Even so, the basic shape of the drama remains tragic in this film. It is as if Mizoguchi means to suggest that the woman who asserts herself in Meiji Japan gains only the freedom of her suffering: she may choose her mode of self-sacrifice, that is all. We see Otoku doing this. Her values change somewhat as she is forced to shift ground in order to survive; but hers is the reward of a heart's true devotion. Thus the pattern of sacrifice is complicated by the addition of an attenuated romance. The object of Otoku's affections, the hero, is Kikunosuke, adopted heir of the Otowaya, one of the most distinguished kabuki families. He rebels against paternal authority, attempts to prove himself, and returns to the bosom of the family a better man. He is not, however, strong on self-discipline. His improvement cannot be made without the help of a heroine far beneath him in status, through much his superior in worldly wisdom and self-control.

The Story of the Last Chrysanthemum explores two courses of action open to Otoku, who begins as the wet nurse for Kikunosuke's younger brother. The first and obvious choice is subjugation to the values represented by kabuki society.

Mizoguchi's choice of this social background for his drama is itself a masterstroke. Kabuki society, with its extreme emphasis on tradition and worse, its resolutely insular world view, harkens back to the rigidities of Japanese feudalism. Thus, kabuki actors cannot succeed on the basis of talent alone: they must be conformists to the nth degree. Their pedigrees must be matched with a spirit of fanatical devotion to the given class structure. Thus, Otoku may be expected to conform to kabuki expectations: she is a servant born and bred, and must accept her lot as a creature entirely subject to the whims of her master.

Against that background and those expectations, Mizoguchi presents his heroine with a second choice: Otoku can challenge the kabuki world and its assumptions. To do this—to show how a lowly maid can prove her individual worth—she helps the ostracized adoptive Kikunosuke train to become a kabuki actor in his own right, quite independently of his father's fame. But this can be possible only by leaving Tokyo where the kabuki theater has too strong a hold. Thus the heroine's choices balance the advantages of stability and inequity against the risks of mobility and equality. Reconciliation of these opposing value systems takes place at the end, but only at Otoku's deathbed.

This melodramatic formula yields a powerful film in *The Story of the Last Chrysanthemum* because Mizoguchi brings to it a style distinctively his own. This can be seen in an encounter between Kikunosuke and Otoku early in the film. Kikunosuke has overheard someone say that theatergoers applaud his kabuki connections, not his performances. He hurries home in a fit of disgust and meets Otoku on the way.

The entire action takes place on a small street bordering a river. It is shot in a single long take. The camera is set considerably lower than street level so that the low-angle shot takes in both characters full length. The camera moves and pauses as they walk and talk. This device directs our attention to the young master's gradually increasing intimacy with the servant, Otoku: the physical distance between them is subtly narrowed. The camera here also immerses us in the serene riverside atmosphere broken from time to time by vendors and their merchandise of rattles and wind-chimes.

Mizoguchi returns to this one-scene, one-shot method time and again, and for the dramatic highlight of the film. As so often, it comes in the final sequence. Kikunosuke, now a famous kabuki actor in his own right, comes to see the dying Otoku. Thematically, the purpose of the scene is to resolve the conflict of values that has given the film its substance. Kikunosuke is a better and a wiser man. He has learned that success (understood as independence) is not its own reward. His fame derives from a combination of independence and dependence; of training and lineage; of what you do and who you are.

It is a moment of truth for Otoku as well. She has proved her worth to the kabuki society which slighted her. We have been witnesses to this—to Kikunosuke's father telling him to go visit his "wife" confined to bed. But this is only a qualified victory. Otoku realizes that she could contribute only part of what Kikunosuke needed to succeed in the kabuki world.

It is important that this final reconciliation of the opposing values takes place in Osaka, not in Tokyo, or any of the other places Kikunosuke has passed through. Tokyo represents the values of conventional kabuki society: wealth, elitism, and insularity. The other places represent the values of drifting: poverty, conniving, and humiliation. Osaka is the kind of place where two such extremes can meet. It is basically a town of merchants—people who value flexibility. The people there can understand kindness to actors. At the same time, they are sharp critics of kabuki performance. Pedigree alone cannot guarantee success in Osaka, as we have seen in an earlier scene where Kikunosuke, while under his uncle Tamizō's protection, was booed by an audience.

Stylistically, distance is maintained by the use of two basic compositions for this final scene: Otoku's bed aligned perpendicular to the camera, with the other character(s) placed to the right or the left; and her bed occupying the screen horizontally. This device creates rhetorical ambivalence, since the moment of climax belongs equally to emotional involvement and intellectual reflection. At first, we find Kikunosuke sitting on the right of Otoku's bed. This shabby quilt bed, almost perpendicular to the camera, is taken from a low-angle, so as to hide Otoku's face occuping the upper half of the screen. However, setting and dialogue speak for her emotion as the opening long shot changes to another long shot of Otoku in bed with Kikunosuke alongside, this time seated to her left. The camera remains fixed on the two for a long time. The wide screen now lets us see more clearly where she is. The shabby room partition, which now comes into view to the left of Kikunosuke, and the equally worn-out *tatami* floor, say enough. The wide screen also emphasizes the low ceilinged room. Otoku, we see, lives in dire poverty in a garret; no sunlight makes its way in through the miniscule window. Closed frame and long take work together to draw us into this atmosphere of felt reality: Otoku has become one with her environment.

Rhythmic flow is effected here by Kikunosuke's bending over Otoku. The nature of Mizoguchi's material here allows for a splendidly effective formalist devic: the composition re-creates a similar one in a dismal inn; only the characters have changed places. Now it is Kikunosuke who echoes Otoku's postures of solicitude, the feminine motions Mizoguchi is so famously sensitive to in his depictions of woman's state of soul. Kikunosuke is uniquely well-qualified to fill this role since his kabuki specialty is female impersonation. Thus Mizoguchi's choice of Hanayagi for this leading man works out brilliantly in combination with the wide-angle long shot. Kikunosuke's shifting emotions—from gratitude to sorrow—can be viewed from afar, without benefit of close-ups.

Otoku's condition is itself enough to create a tearful atmosphere. This climax becomes lachrymose, thanks to a cicada's chirping introduced twice on the sound track. This familiar *haiku* seasonal signifier evokes the particular sentiment associated with the mutability of human affairs (*mujō*). It already predicts Otoku's approaching death, which will ironically take place at the height of summer, the time of most exuberant life force.

The pathos of Otoku's death is expressed more dramatically through intercutting between contrasting scenes: shots of Otoku accompanied by the landlord's daughter are interspersed with long or medium shots of Kikunosuke in the stern of a boat heading a gorgeous procession. His boat glides horizontally or diagonally across the screen. Here Mizoguchi makes the most of open framing in order to convey a sense of the long stretch of river the parade occupies. We immediately perceive that the event will last too long for Kikunosuke to be present at his wife's death.

As expected, Mizoguchi cuts to Otoku's deathbed. The joyous orchestral music of flute and chimes which she has heard coming from the parade accentuates the solemnity of her death. The girl's piercing cry, "Don't die!" is again overtaken by the festival music when we enter the final coda.

Kikunosuke is now facing the camera, standing in the boat. He bows right and left, obviously to the spectators (out of frame). The shot size grows larger until the final close-up (never very close) shows him looking straight into the camera, then bowing. Like the shocking close-up of Ayako's face at the end of *Osaka Elegy*, this single shot is somewhat baffling. Mizoguchi puts us in the position of spectators watching Kikunosuke's parade. But unlike spectators blindly adoring this celebrity, we are in a more precarious situation: we know all about his circumstances. Are we supposed to feel for this actor who must pretend to be happy despite the loss of his wife? Or are we expected to feel indignant, seeing only the male who thrives on female sacrifice? Kikunosuke's face is too impassive to provide a clue. Mizoguchi leaves this rhetorical ambiguity for us to resolve.

Troubles in a Troubled World: The Trilogy Incomplete

The Story of the Last Chrysanthemum won Mizoguchi an Education Ministry Award and the chance to serve on the National Film Committee. His depression had vanished. He had every reason to believe that this recent success could be crowned by two more films dealing with the world of traditional theater.

In July 1940, he started work on the second fim in the proposed trilogy, *Naniwa Onna* (*The Woman of Osaka*). This was his first incursion into the world of *bunraku,* or traditional puppet theater. Here, his inspiration was to invest the heroine Ochika with a powerful personality. Unlike his previous heroines, she exemplifies strong-willed wisdom and leadership.

Mizoguchi cast this leading role with his usual care, and his choice of Kinuyo Tanaka led to one of the happiest personal and professional relationships of his life. From the start, he was surprised by Tanaka's enthusiasm and patience, just as she was impressed by his authority and sense of purpose. She became the leading lady in most of his subsequent films, including award-winners like *Ugetsu* and *The Life of Oharu.*

Mizoguchi remained Platonically in love with Tanaka till the day he died. His attitude toward her revealed an interesting aspect of his complex personality: a kind of childlike innocence. Mizoguchi was promiscuous, but only with "professional" women. Toward others, he was capable of naive, open, boyish admiration.

According to contemporary accounts, *The Woman of Osaka* was a fair success (the print is now lost). The early forties, however, were difficult times for the film industry in Japan. The political and economic stresses created by military expansion brought severe restrictions. The maximum playing time at a regular theater, for example, was cut to three hours. Footage was limited to 4,500 meters for a silent film and 5,000 meters for a talkie. Subject matter was heavily censored.

By the time Mizoguchi began work on the last part of his trilogy, *Geidō Ichidai Otoko (The Life of an Actor,* 1941), his company was feeling less supportive. The script, which dealt with the life of an illegitimate son of a kabuki actor, was considered inappropriate for audiences exposed to wartime conditions. Faced with this response, Mizoguchi's enthusiasm waned and the resulting work (whose print is lost) was considered markedly inferior to the other films in his trilogy.

5

Wartime and Samurai Films (1941–45)

War and Censorship

BY 1941, even the uncompromising Mizoguchi had to find a way to cooperate with the wartime government. This he managed to do by taking on a new and challenging subject for him: the samurai film. He was hoping to escape the demand for artistic jingoism by turning to traditional materials with popular appeal. Most of his countrymen were familiar with idealized depictions of the samurai virtues of loyalty, honor, and frugality in fiction, plays, and films about feudal Japan, so he had every reason to expect success, even in the face of competition from wartime propaganda hits with titles like *Moyuru Ōzora (The Great Burning Sky,* 1940).

A ready-made hit subject presented itself in the form of a play enjoying success on the stage just then: *Mayama Chūshingura,* a version of the historical tale of forty-seven ronin, or masterless samurai, who sacrifice themselves to avenge the disgrace and death of their lord. This tale—familiar to every Japanese child—had provided a cinema box office hit as early as 1918, and had been refilmed a number of times. Mizoguchi, as usual, was undaunted by the success of other directors. He was clearly set on joining their number, even as he denied having any special ambitions for his film.[1]

From the start, he gave himself astonishing scope, as did the Shōchiku Company. An independent production company was formed to deal with the monumental demands of this picture. An out-size replica of a part of Edo Castle, for example, was commissioned and built at a cost twice that of any ordinary film.

Mizoguchi's magnificent self-confidence and epic ambitions were checked, however, as soon as shooting began. As so often before, he was stymied by unfamiliar themes and historical backgrounds. Even the samurai ethos, which so many others found so accessible, seemed to elude his grasp.[2] Halfway through the shooting, he was so demoralized

63

op) In The Loyal 47 Ronin, Part I *(1941), Ōishi (Chōjūrō*
‹warazaki, right) bids farewell to Lord Asano (Yoshizaburō
‾ashi) on his way to execution; (bottom) the swordsman
‹usashi (Chōjūrō Kawarazaki, second from left) in Musashi
‹iyamoto (1944).

that he seemed to have lost his gift for composition and for giving forceful direction. Yet he persisted. Then, during the filming of part 2, his wife suddenly went insane. Not even that was allowed to interrupt shooting, not even for a day.

At last *The Loyal 47 Ronin: Part 1* was completed. It was a qualified artistic success and a distinct commercial failure. Its release date a week before Pearl Harbor was particularly unfortunate. In any case, wartime audiences soon proved indifferent to the blandishments of historical pageantry. The two executives held responsible for the exorbitant cost of Mizoguchi's film were forced to resign and its special production company dissolved. Work did, however, continue on part 2, which opened in February the following year with similar indifferent success.

Genroku Chūshingura (The Loyal 47 Ronin, 1941–42)

Mizoguchi's version of this classic tale had all the advantages of the "great" motion picture: familiar plot and character motivation; scenic and visual splendor; and authentic performances by actors well-versed in the ethos of one of a nation's most glorious epochs. Yet both parts failed with audiences and critics.

Traditional expectations had something to do with it. After all, the story deals with forty-seven swashbucklers who plot and execute a magnificent and suicidal revenge for their lord's disgrace and death. The previous film versions had in common, for example, a spectacular climax on the taking of the *ronins*' vow. Mizoguchi consistently neglects the operatic conventions of the piece. His approach is strangely static and formal, and in places downright pedantic. "Ceremonial" might be the word to express the effect of his (we see now) characteristically personal focus on his material. He wants to get behind the blood and thunder to the meaning of the vow—its cost in inner conflict between *giri* and *ninjō*, between duty and personal inclination.[3]

His choice of original text also enforces a difference. Previous directors had used a kabuki play, *Kanadehon Chūshingura*, which studies motivation leading to dramatic action: what reasons lead Lord Asano to commit lese majesty, drawing on Lord Kira; what makes his faithful retainers determine to sacrifice their lives in pursuit of a vendetta?

Mizoguchi's source, the kabuki play *Mayama Chūshingura*, is rather more cerebral. It studies motivation in relation to manners and morals, in high-flown feudal language, in nineteen acts. One high point deals with the fine points of vendetta ritual; another questions the propriety of plotting revenge at the same time that an appeal for legal redress is being made through official channels.

Mizoguchi is not afraid to add to such heady stuff. His screenplay includes comment on the possibility that a vendetta carried out for reasons of loyalty may not constitute a crime of disrespect to the emperor. Even so, the resolutely elevated tone of his version works paradoxically to forge an intense, emotional bond between the viewer and the characters on the screen. As so often, he puts the camera in charge, taking full advantage of crane shots, dollying, long takes and shots (rather than close-ups) for a synergy of form and content. This is most successful in scenes depicting crises of separation as characters torn between social obligation and personal feelings calmly do the terrible things demanded of them by duty.

The opening five-minute sequence shows Mizoguchi's stylistic excellence. It is filmed in five shots, but Mizoguchi takes such care with continuity that we enjoy the impression of seeing one long take. This is characteristic of his approach throughout. (The total length of this two-part film is three hours and thirty-five minutes. Mizoguchi gives 160 shots of, on the average, 80 seconds each.)[4]

One of the most astonishing instances of synthesis of form and content depicts the condemned Lord Asano meeting his faithful retainer Ōishi on the way to the courtyard where Asano will submit to ritual *seppuku*. The tense ceremonial aspect of the occasion is heightened by the white wall dominating the screen. An extreme high angle shot shows Asano in white (the color of death in Japan) moving diagonally along the wall from the upper left of the screen. He meets Ōishi kneeling by the gate. The camera tracks steadily up to them as Asano expresses his gratitude for this show of loyalty. Very few words are exchanged, but the cherry tree in blossom behind Ōishi conveys a larger message clearly: it is the traditional image associated with mortality at the height of the samurai's youth.

Asano enters the gate, which is shut to exclude Ōishi. The screen is charged with the emotional overtones of separation. The camera moves up the wall to show Asano, the only moving figure, advancing to his death in the courtyard. This raising of the camera is clearly felt as a sympathetic gesture to the loyal retainer who has been denied access to the last moments of the lord.

As may be expected, the male world of the samurai gives Mizoguchi some excellent opportunities to display his expertise in portraying female self-sacrifice. In fact, he deals with the crises of three women whose styles of suffering vary according to the class they were born to suffer in.

The first is Lady Asano receiving the news of her husband's death. The camera moves in a series of shots that suggest a suitable deference to the rigid formality of this very personal crisis. First we see a number of ladies-in-waiting bowing. Then the camera follows two attendants up to Lady Asano. We see her from the back, sitting bolt upright; her very posture speaks for the strain of controlling her emotions which, of course, she does. The camera comes to a sudden halt. This is the *merihari* device, a kabuki convention whereby a sudden halting of the actor's gesture leads to a decisive action. Here, the camera marks a moment of decision: Lady Asano will cut her long hair, a gesture of complete self-abnegation as she prepares to enter a cloister. The camera pans back round the ladies-in-waiting as they cover their faces with their wide sleeves in a well-born gesture expressive of great emotion.

The samurai wife must suffer the loss of her husband before his actual death. Her duty is to seek divorce in order to free him to fulfill the suicidal pledge to avenge his lord. Again, the externals of the scene are formal. Riku, Ōishi's wife, waits by the partition wall of their living room. He enters. She closes the partition and joins him framed in the center of the room. This time the camera holds steady; the one-scene, one-shot approach invites us to consider the more intimate relationship behind the grave formality of the occasion. Riku asks for a divorce. Ōishi tells her to take their younger children and go to her parents. As the Japanese audience knows, the samurai ethos forbids effusive words or motions on either side as the husband accepts the wife's sacrifice. She is putting duty (*giri*) before personal inclination (*ninjō*); her husband's gratitude is expressed only in his telling her to take care of herself. Yet the pathos of this scene is keenly felt, even as Mizoguchi limits its lyrical expressiveness to a concluding fade.

The conflict between *giri* and *ninjō* is more openly dealt with in the case of the plebian woman who has loved a samurai. Such a woman's grasp of upper-class proprieties will itself be imperfect, and her inclinations to express conflicting emotions correspondingly stronger. Even duty's claims on her will be problematic because of her social origins, so that in the end she becomes more like a victim of love in a melodrama than a model of womanly self-sacrifice.

This woman's conflict begins with doubts about personal inclination itself. Omino has been the lover of Isogai, one of Ōishi's fellow ronin. Moreover, she has been useful in plotting the vendetta. Now that the forty-seven ronin lie under sentence of death, she wants to know if she really is Isogai's beloved—or just a tool.

The scenario for her crisis is significantly more complex than the other two. She comes to Ōishi in disguise, begging him to serve as her intermediary. Mizoguchi changes a reverse-field shot of the two alone to a long take showing them seated on either side of a brazier. The composition is varied by Ōishi leaving and returning with Isogai; then the camera draws back to fit all three figures into the frame.

Clearly, the focus here is not on any one of the three, but rather on their subtly different responses to the conflict between *giri* and *ninjō*. The irreconcilable nature of duty and personal inclination is given more pointed emphasis in this scenario. Omino, acting in character as a commoner, but out of samurai code, demands to know the nature of Isogai's feelings for her. He pretends not to know her—*giri* demands total commitment to his lord on this eve of honorable death. Nevertheless, Ōishi intervenes to strike a precarious balance. He orders Isogai to produce a *koto* plectrum (pick) he has in his possession. This keepsake, given by Omino, speaks for his devotion. Now, Ōishi explains, it is up to her to let her lover go in peace to die like a samurai. Omino is left alone to express her grief in the characteristic Mizoguchi style of letting body language do the work of close-ups. Her candid postures are in character, but they strike a jarring note in a film whose tone throughout is resolutely elevated.

Worse yet, the climax of this near-masterpiece is flawed by intercutting Omino's suicide with that of the forty-seven ronin. One understands why Mizoguchi was accused of not really understanding the samurai ethos. This scene could also be taken as evidence of the director's reverting to type: Mizoguchi giving us yet another masterly depiction of the sacrificed woman's sufferings. Or else, one might see him yielding to wartime pressures after all, giving the long-suffering women of militarist Japan their place alongside the warriors dying honorably abroad.

In any case, the failure of this film left Mizoguchi free to relapse into idleness and depression, which he did with a vengeance for eighteen months. Then, as before, he tried the working cure. The result was another mediocre film about kabuki actors: *Danjūrō Sandai (Three Generations of Danjūrō,* 1944). The best that can be said for this film is that it stands alongside Kurosawa's *The Most Beautiful* as one of the most tightly structured efforts of that terrible year for Japanese cinema, 1944.

Samurai "Action" Films: *Miyamoto Musashi (Musashi Miyamoto,* 1944) and *Meitō Bijomaru, (The Famous Sword of Bijomaru,* 1944)

No survey of Mizoguchi's unhappy wartime period would be complete without mention of his two entirely forgettable samurai "action" films.

The hero Musashi Miyamoto was a box office draw when Mizoguchi took him on. He represents the impetuous swordsman whose weapon figures in a quest for what later generations would call personal integration. His guru is a Zen monk who helps temper raw courage with feats of meditation—in one instance by tying Musashi overnight in a tree. It follows that Musashi must fight a climactic duel with an opponent almost every bit his equal. Romantic interest is provided by a subplot, about a heroine who follows her fiancé as he roams the countryside encountering adventures during his quest.

Mizoguchi's version ignores all these thrills save the final test of swordsmanship. His Musashi is more mature and genuinely accomplished throughout—a fit subject for tests more subtle than feats of derring-do. Yet Mizoguchi fails to build to a climax at the end where other directors, more sure of the common touch, managed to achieve effects still worth looking at.

On the whole, this film looks like another casualty of wartime censorship.[5] Certainly no Musashi picture which explored the man-woman relationship Mizoguchi-style had a chance of being approved. Perhaps this film shows what a misguided spirit of compromise could do for a master like Mizoguchi. For example, there is the climax of edification arranged for a young admirer Shinobu. Contrary to his avowed belief that "to use perfect swordsmanship for the purpose of revenge is contrary to the code of the samurai," Musashi has served as fencing instructor for this girl's brother bent on avenging their father's death. After her brother dies in her arms of wounds received in that cause, Shinobu seeks sympathy from their instructor/champion. She finds Musashi in a temple intent on carving the image of a saint. His austere concentration warns her not to intrude on this variation of the quest. The camera cross-cuts officiously, drawing the obvious parallel between Musashi's devotion to Buddha and Shinobu's devoutly distant admiration of it. The obligatory moon looms overhead. An orchestra steals in. Even a gong sounds, merging with the carver's chisel strokes to indicate time passing—and the heroic duration of this spell. The effect is ludicrous, a mere perfunctory juggling of conventional symbols.

Much the same thing happens, to even worse effect, in Mizoguchi's other "action" samurai film, *The Famous Sword Bijomaru*. Our disappointment is keener here because he makes nothing at all of material that is so resonant with meaning in his films of the 1930s and again in the 1950s.

The subject this time is a swordsmith, Kiyone. The weapon he has made as an important ceremonial offering breaks when its owner's life depends on it. This shameful reflection on Kiyone's craftsmanship calls for ritual suicide—or public atonement through the forging of a better sword.

To this is added a typical Mizoguchi theme: a woman's encouragement of her wavering hero's commitment to his goal. Here the woman is Sasae, daughter of the man undone by the defective sword. Better yet, her devotion is reciprocated in the end: Kiyone forges a redemptive weapon that can slice a helmet of steel in two—and gives it as a token of grateful affection and admiration to Sasae, so that she can avenge the death of her father.

Even this combination fails to engage Mizoguchi's interest and imagination. The film wanders from effect to effect in its search for dramatic high points. As Kiyone forges the master weapon (Bijomaru), his helper faints away exhausted while he continues on alone with the endless hammering. He grows mortally weary, and as music joins hammer clang we expect a climax. Instead, we see Sasae's image superimposed on the screen—not once, but three times before the smith achieves the finished product.

Obviously, Sasae is to be seen as a source of inner strength, a kindly ghostly muse. Mizoguchi will use her like again, but brilliantly, in *Ugetsu*. Here, however, she offers no real moral resonance, no richness of characterization.

Worse follows in the final scene—where Mizoguchi so often says too much. Sasae's revenge is complete; the way is clear to a happy ending. She and Kiyone glide downriver in a tiny boat, like commonplace lovers in an amusement park. Even the music fits the parting conventional shot. The happy pair gaze deep into one another's eyes. He tells her that the sword Bijomaru is to be her keepsake, her pledge of security. She is appropriately maiden shy. The viewer thinks ruefully of the Mizoguchi so richly inventive, elsewhere, of codas genuinely resonant with feeling and meaning.

6

Facing the Occupation: Films about Women's Liberation (1946–49)

The Occupation Period

ON 15 AUGUST 1945, Mizoguchi, then in Kyoto, heard the news of Japan's surrender to the Allied Forces. "He was in a state of shock over Japan's defeat and felt that he did not know what the world was coming to."[1]

One of the democratic policies which the Allied Forces tried to enforce was the consolidation of labor unions, including those in the film industry. The conservative Mizoguchi, who was extremely shy about talking in public, was elected president of the first labor union organized at the Shōchiku Ōfuna Studio. However, he found himself unfit for the job, since he "was the kind of union president who wanted to stop a strike."[2] Moreover, when the war was over, there were few directors left at the Shōchiku Ōfuna Studio. Mizoguchi hated to see film production crippled by a series of strikes. He resigned his post after three months in office and went to work making films. Sensitive to current trends, however, Mizoguchi made *Josei no Shōri (The Victory of Women*, 1946), one of his strongest "feminist" films.

Josei no Shōri (The Victory of Women, 1946)

The best way to approach *The Victory of Women*, Mizoguchi's outspoken celebration of women's rights, would be to demonstrate how poorly he fared in pursuing this subject. As we have seen, his prewar films were structured around women's confrontation with a male-dominated, money-oriented society; similarly, in this first postwar film, he explores that theme but in a somewhat different context—the changing society.

Mizoguchi shows basically two alternate methods of adapting to the world through the polarization of his characters. The heroine Hiroko, an attorney, stands for female independence while her elder sister, Michiko, is initially portrayed as content with the submissive role of

ımaro and His Five Women: *the famous* Ukiyo *printmaker*
nosuke Bandō) and one of his models, the tragic heroine
ita (Kinuyo Tanaka).

71

women. This bifurcation in values is made more distinct by the opposition of two male characters. Hiroko's fiancé, Yamaoka, who served long terms of imprisonment during the war as a leader in the pacifist movement, encourages her to work for the welfare of helpless female defendants; Kōno, Michiko's husband, who sentenced Yamaoka to prison, is a strong male chauvinist, and believes that a woman's place is in the home.

One of the greatest flaws in the film is that Hiroko and the two male characters are rigidly stereotyped. From the outset, they become, as it were, mere mouthpieces for political maxims and textbook illustrations. Yamaoka, confined to a hospital after his release from prison, speaks to reporters: "The military regime warped the masses. My slogan is to be completely absorbed in democracy and let it be mine." Kōno, faced with the democratization of the judicial system, defends his conservative stance: "Public servants are public servants. The masses are the masses." Hiroko, whom Mizoguchi undoubtedly fails to draw fully, is also inflexible; she is intolerant of anything that runs counter to the new democracy: "The feudal law made men its tool. However, law must be human in that it derives from our understanding of the human condition."

The two value systems are brought into formal conflict when Kōno and Hiroko come together in court as prosecutor and defense attorney respectively. Tomo Asakura, a former classmate of Hiroko, has been brought to trial for infanticide: she has smothered her child rather than let it suffer a life of extreme poverty and degradation. Michiko brings some mobility to this drama of conflicting values because she shows how even the woman who finds herself "in place" in the home begins to shift her ground. In the end she abandons the double role of dutiful wife and daughter-in-law.

Yet Mizoguchi's delineation of Michiko posits another troublesome aspect. Her moral quandary is placed in a typical melodramatic situation without any insight into what prompts her to act with such sudden decisiveness. We are left with the impression that this would-be radical transformation is a way out of the classical dilemma between *giri* and *ninjō*: her obligation to husband and mother-in-law, and her feelings for a sister whom both despise. Her growing awareness of female oppression does not seem to be a result of any self-learning process grounded in direct experience. Her vision is too limited to see her suffering or the suffering of a woman like Tomo as a representation of the suffering of the masses. Michiko merely trades one mold for another: she moves from the rigidities of traditional submissiveness to the orthodoxies of her sister's "liberation." Thus, in the end, we are bewildered by so radical a change: Mizoguchi lets Michiko cry out after the trial of the mother who has killed her child: "The most fortunate woman in the world is the one

Tomo (Mitsuko Mito, left) in The Victory of Women *confesses her crime of infanticide to Hiroko (Kinuyo Tanaka), an ex-classmate who is now a lawyer.*

who can stand by herself. I am no longer a member of the weaker sex. I am no longer dependent on men."

The extension of personal confrontation between sister and brother-in-law to a public level is another melodramatic device. This leads to a disappointing climactic moment in the court-room scene. Here Mizoguchi's camera work is far from subtle. He simply uses a close-up of Hiroko occupying the center of the screen as she loudly declares that the defendant is a victim of the military regime which deprived her husband of life. Perhaps Mizoguchi's intention is to show quite plainly the strength and dignity of Hiroko, despite the death of her fiancé during the trial—another melodramatic convenience. But style and issues collaborate too obviously to evoke a rich response.

As Tadao Satō points out, during the trial we are denied access to Tomo's thought.[3] All she does is weep. We begin to wonder if she has any self-awareness at all and whether she wants to be saved or punished. Similar doubts are inspired by Michiko's sudden declaration of independence. We wonder how a woman so demure, so conditioned by a lifetime of traditional submission, can actually become economically independent.

The film ends with a view of Hiroko on her way to hear the verdict. With a look of firm determination on her face, she walks straight into the camera to the sound of music. Yet this assertiveness is undercut by our impression that the film does not really lead to a stable vision of female emancipation and that it has left out many complex issues inherent in the social context.

As Junichirō Tanaka points out, filmmaking after the war entailed great difficulties: increasing inflation, shortages of every kind, including a real and painful scarcity of foodstuffs.[4] Paradoxically, these miseries worked to the advantage of the movie industry. The public, eager to escape them, and freed from a long period of military oppression, streamed into the theaters that had survived the bombings. In order to meet this demand, the film industry hastened to build more theaters and push for new productions—real entertainment in place of policy films.

Mizoguchi, too, was forced into mass-production. At the same time he was anxious to surpass his fellow directors, who were bent on making box office hits. Among them were Ozu, Kinoshita, and Yoshimura. Mizoguchi decided to make his mark with a new theme. Instead of turning to melodrama, then being revived in Japan, he embarked on a film with a feudal setting, *Utamaro o Meguru Gonin no Onna* (*Utamaro and His Five Women*, 1946).

It was extremely difficult to make a period-genre film during the Occupation because the headquarters of the Allied Powers heavily censored those feudal elements which, they thought, ran counter to democratic ideas. Mizoguchi had to go to Allied headquarters and argue for what he considered the antifeudal nature of his film: "Utamaro was a liberal artist who appealed to the common man." The resulting film was not a success. Kaneto Shindō characterizes it as a dry film, lacking in sensuality.[5] Mizoguchi had had to sacrifice his artistic integrity in order to promote democratic issues; and as always, he lost out in a situation requiring compromise.

Utamaro o Meguru Gonin no Onna (*Utamaro and His Five Women*, 1946)

Though not a negligible work, *Utamaro and His Five Women* is a mediocre contribution by a great director. Unlike *Sisters of the Gion* and *The Story of the Last Chrysanthemum*, it fails to invite reflection on issues of female existence seen in a larger sociocultural context. *Utamaro and His Five Women* is a conventional outspoken statement in celebration of men and women trying to achieve some measure of personal freedom within the restrictive framework of feudal Japanese society. It was a theme welcome in the heady, "democratic" days of the postwar period. The trouble is that Mizoguchi's highly personal style tends to elevate itself above the rather simplistic content of the screenplay. Yet this film, like most of Mizoguchi's, has its fine moments. Instead of the kabuki actor or samurai warrior as the feudal protagonist, we have Utamaro Kitagawa, the famous woodblock print artist. Naturally, he chooses to assert his freedom in a limited sense: in order to fulfill his artistic mission, he will depict beautiful women. The film shows how the artist's contact with one man and five women leads to experiences illustrating the value of self-fulfillment.

Naturally, female emancipation in the twentieth-century sense is not possible for these women of Utamaro's time, but they do emancipate themselves. For example, the courtesan Takasode, who has modeled for Utamaro, obeys her feelings and elopes with her lover. Another model, Oran, refuses to be the mere plaything of a wealthy feudal lord; she moves, in fact, down in the social scale by eloping with an artist apprentice from the samurai class. Yukie, the epitome of innocence and refinement, has been brought up as the daughter of the head of a distinguished Kanō school of painting; she challenges the values of her father by leaving home to be closer to her fiancé. Oshin, another courtesan, the only comic stereotype, moves from forced confinement to willing bondage; she completes her term of service within the Yoshihara pleasure quarters and chooses to marry Utamaro's servant-apprentice. Though this is another form of confinement in a male-oriented society, it is nonetheless commitment to freedom for her.

Okita, the most extreme of these women, is given the most complete portrait. She fights feudal oppression with a passion. Finding herself rejected by her fickle, weak lover (the typical Mizoguchi male), she stabs both him and her rival, who, incidentally, is Takasode.

The film is marred by the director's apparent indecisiveness. Our attention is shifted too frequently from one case history to another. The women experience their awakening without focusing our attention on what must be the unifying theme of the film: Utamaro's moral and artistic dilemma as an artist.

One of the finest scenes, in pictorial terms, shows the artist at work. The camera is artfully tilted to take in candlelight reflecting off the room partitions in sharply contrasting black and white. Many sheets of paper are shown scattered around the room when the servant-apprentice lights the candle. The message is clear, yet the scene fails to realize its potential for insight into the artist's struggle against failure to achieve the print he has in mind.

What, then, are the merits of this compromised film? Its outstanding strength certainly lies in the director's cinematic expertise in single compositions. The film begins with a brilliant example. The camera moves slowly in contrary motion to a procession of courtesans shown against blossoming cherry trees. The effect of the entire two-minute take, which consists of two shots, is that of the one-scene, one-shot method. We hardly notice the cut precisely because of the flow of the two parties and the extremely long look of the camera during the first shot. As one of the spectators says, "This is a Harunobu print."

The fusion of the gorgeously attired courtesans accompanied by little girls with cherry blossoms is indeed evocative of the mood associated with "the floating world" (*ukiyo*), the Japanese equivalent of *carpe diem* sensuality and eroticism. Interestingly, the crossing of the camera and the procession does not create an effect of speeding up. Rather, it creates the impression of groups of similarly dressed courtesans floating downstream, one after another. The horizontal flow is subtly balanced by the vertical flow of the characters as each lowers her body ceremoniously at a regular interval during the procession. Are these women from the fashionable pleasure quarters of Yoshihara, though distinguished in their own profession, as happy and joyous as the spectators? Their faces under the thick coat of makeup are motionless; they may be thought to display a touch of resignation to the fate of female existence—playthings of men. However, Mizoguchi finalizes our first perception of a collective sense of sorrow in this class of women by shifting a long shot to an extremely short, medium shot singling out one courtesan, Takasode.

Throughout the film we are also amazed by the pervasiveness of the one-scene, one-shot method. Mizoguchi makes the most of Japanese architecture, which enables him to deploy his camera freely without cutting. For example, he relies heavily upon the sliding room partitions which can be easily opened and closed, the long corridor connecting many rooms, and the white *shōji* door which can display an individual character's action in silhouette.

One such scene depicts Okita's confrontation with Takasode after the latter has eloped with the fickle Shōzaburō. The episode begins with a medium shot in a small country cottage of Takasode trimming her toenails. The room opens onto a veranda/corridor. The camera pulls back as Okita appears to the spectator's left and sits in the open space, demanding her lover of Takasode. The camera continues to roll in a fixed position, giving a deep focus to the interior, especially the open *shōji* door occupying the upper right of the screen. After Okita starts searching for Shōzaburō, this door serves as the focus for the comings and goings of both women.

Special emphasis is laid on the relative postures of the two women. At the start of their confrontation, Takasode stands against a pillar, a conventional prop giving vertical weight to the composition, while Okita sits at the edge of the corridor. They then wrestle, standing around the pillar, before Okita moves off on her search of the house while Takasode sits down indifferently. Toward the end of their quarrel, they are presented singly: Takasode picking up her straw sandals, bending down to a steppingstone as she leaves; Okita, after a brief view of the empty house, returning to search the premises once more.

Perhaps one of the finest instances in which the one-scene, one-shot method is integrated with issues of female existence is the climatic moment which follows Okita's murder of Shōzaburō and Takasode. A medium shot of her exhausted, with disheveled hair, opens the scene. Again, the corridor leading to Utamaro's living room serves as the background when Okita crosses it. The slightly tilted camera is an obvious index of Okita's emotional disarray. Utamaro and others then cross the corridor. The camera pans along, then follows him as he enters the living room. Okita sits down, followed by Utamaro, Oman (Okita's maid), and Yukie. The closed frame provided by the *shōji* door, along with a high-angle shot, forcibly concentrates our attention on this pressing situation.

Okita now verbally justifies her pursuit of passion: "There's no choice because I did not want to deceive myself in love." Her action is a personal triumph, a consummation of pure passion. For the first time, the two women in her presence—Yukie and Oman—realize what tragic passion means. The camera keeps moving at a fixed position, but a deep focus on Yukie and then on Oman during each woman's moment of insight brings a slight textural change.

From this point on, the camera's gaze becomes more assertive. To indicate the subtle bond established between Okita and Utamaro through his portrait of her, the camera moves slightly back and forth between them, as Okita exclaims: "Please be nice to my portrait after I die."

There is no compositional awkwardness here. When Okita stands, the camera moves to keep her in frame. Then we see a close-up of Okita's face—one of the rare close-ups in this film. This suggests full exposure to Okita's resignation to fate together with her personal victory through strength of character. A close-up continues as the camera's long gaze remains on Okita, who moves to the pillar in the corridor and says, "You've been good to me," then disappears.

The short presentation of the empty hallway with the pillar occupying the center, as if it were a definite separation between Okita to be executed (death) and her survivors (life), offers the viewer a moment for contemplative repose. The women cross the corridor hurriedly, following Okita. Then the camera moves to the left to show Utamaro left alone in the living room.

The way this scene ends is uncharacteristic of Mizoguchi, who is generally credited with rich shades of meaning. Here, he relies on a straightforward message from the artist Utamaro still in handcuffs: "I want to draw. I want to draw so badly." The film's obvious message is that both Okita and Utamaro are finally united by "passion" as Okita's consummation of love free from social constraint restores Utamaro's creative urge. However, precisely because of its conventional "democratic" overtone, this conclusion seems more like an empty echo than a genuine outcry of Utamaro's surge of emotion.

Immediately after the completion of *Utamaro and His Five Women,* Mizoguchi was called back to Tokyo for his next project: *Joyū Sumako no Koi (The Love of Sumako the Actress,* 1947). Once again, he worked with the veteran scriptwriter, Yoshikata Yoda. Mizoguchi was desperate by this time to escape from his own "mannerisms." Shōchiku's rival, the Tōhō Company, was also making a film about Sumako Matsui, entitled *Joyū (Actress)* with the veteran director Teinosuke Kinugasa. Mizoguchi, moved by the spirit of emulation, bombarded Yoda with letters giving detailed instructions.

Joyū Sumako no Koi (The Love of Sumako the Actress, 1947)

This film is cast in the same mold as *The Victory of Women* and *Utamaro and His Five Women.* It is an assertion of the need for human emancipation. However, this time Mizoguchi pursues a similar theme in a different cultural and social climate: the theatrical world of conventional Meiji society.

The hero and the heroine are the scholar/director Hōgetsu Shimamura and the actress Sumako Matsui. Both made an enormous contribution to the Shingeki (New Drama) Movement—a movement toward the Western-style realism of playwrights such as Ibsen and Chekhov. This film posits two values between which Hōgetsu and Sumako must choose: conformity and liberation. For Sumako conformity means submitting to the role of wife and mother, and this is certainly unacceptable to her. As emancipated as Nora in *A Doll's House,* she leaves two husbands and chooses to live on the stage, free to love Hōgetsu, who leaves his wife and daughter for her.

Hōgetsu's case poses a more complex problem of male emancipation. He is doubly bound by a sense of *giri.* Domestically, he is shackled by the manners and conventions of the household of a distinguished scholar into which he has married. Both his wife and mother-in-law expect him to honor the respectable traditional family. Professionally, respect for and loyalty to his superior, Shōyō Tsubouchi (a leading Shaksperian scholar in the Meiji era) keeps him from effecting any radical change in the New Drama Movement.

Like *The Story of the Last Chrysanthemum*, Mizoguchi's telling of this story moves away from conformity to roaming and then finally back to reconciliation. The opening sequence maps out this course of action. We see Hōgetsu lecturing on Ibsen's plays to a class of eager students: "The struggle between living honestly and the bitter reality of human society is the core of the modern drama created by Ibsen. . . ." Ironically, Hōgetsu is like Nora in Ibsen's *A Doll's House*. First, he must reject the values represented by all that his status as an adopted son-in-law implies. Living purely, "honestly," means rejecting convention—and the same goes for contemporary drama, which he aims to liberate. He takes his cue from those who say "Art imitates life—and vice versa," and proceeds to repudiate the values of his authoritative teacher/superior.

Meaningful professional commitment resulting from domestic freedom cannot be found in Tokyo, a city where acquaintances can accuse Hōgetsu and Sumako of breach of good conduct. So after forming Geijutsuza (the Art Group), they travel through Japan and even to Manchuria, to live in a manner they consider true to life and art. They derive a sense of strength and adequacy from this shift in values regardless of the hardships imposed on them by it.

In the end, the ostracized lovers are reconciled with the professional establishment, though not with their families. Shōyō and his followers are forced to acknowledge that Hōgetsu and Sumako have succeeded in bringing the New Drama Movement to the masses. Yet Hōgetsu's wife and mother-in-law never forgive him for breaking up the "distinguished" family. However, Hōgetsu and Sumako's implementation of personal assertiveness and meaningful commitment is short-lived because the film ends in a typically melodramatic fashion—the death of Hōgetsu in middle age and the suicide of Sumako who finds her life unfulfilled without him.

Interestingly enough, Mizoguchi employs a conventional style in this equally conventional narrative context. The most consistent aspect throughout is the use of the long take for most scenes. One such scene depicts the death of Hōgetsu. His body lies on a quilt occupying the lower portion of the screen. Nakamura, Hōgetsu's colleague, is in the center, facing a little stand with the incense container on it. Shōyō, who has just arrived, is on the left while Sumako is sitting on the right. The camera is so stable that little gestures like Sumako and Nakamura bowing slightly to Shōyō do not go unnoticed. As Sumako and Shōyō move on their knees to Nakamura, the alignment of their gathering close together becomes so symmetrical that it richly transmits the shared sentiment of the sorrow and austerity of death.

Even in shooting performances on stage—Tolstoy's *Resurrection*, Ibsen's *A Doll's House*, and Maeterlinck's *Magda*—medium shots of the performers are consistently alternated with long shots of the audience. Together, these conventional perspectives discourage our attempts to consider the film's rhetorical effect.

The only instance where we see variations of shot-size and angles is in Sumako's final performance of *Carmen*, which anticipates her suicide. We see a rare close-up of Carmen's face. A medium shot of Carmen climbing the stairs followed by Jose yields to a reverse angle shot of him still on the stairs pleading for her love. Mizoguchi even shows a shot from the wings of Jose trying to kill Carmen. The scene ends with a close-up of her corpse lying at his feet. Here, control of the camera is notably unrestricted in comparison to what went before. Even though Sumako is acting in performance, we sense quite naturally that something deeply personal is taking place inside her. Another close-up provides an unhappy soap-operatic moment. We are shown the face of Sumako, this time lying in her casket, surrounded by flowers, while the orchestra plays "Life Is Short" (a song sung by Watanabe in the cabaret in the famous night-town sequence in Kurosawa's *Ikiru*).

The Love of Sumako the Actress was financially successful, but compared with Kinugasa's version, it lacked both depth and organization. Yoda claims that its artistic failure was due to a poor scenario; he felt that it did not succeed in exploring the personalities of the intellectual Hōgetsu and the actress Sumako.[6] However, the element of compromise is surely much to blame. The Shōchiku management would not allow Mizoguchi to deal with the obviously questionable character of Sumako, lest the sensibilities of the audience be outraged. Instead, he was forced to give the public what it wanted: a sympathetic heroine in a conventional melodrama.

No wonder Mizoguchi found it difficult to break out of his serious depression. He looked around feverishly for a "break-through" theme. He found it in *Yoru no Onnatachi (Women of the Night*, 1948). He was now fifty years old, very much the man to turn his back on past failure and give himself heart and soul to the next opportunity.

Yoru no Onnatachi (Women of the Night, 1948)

In *Women of the Night*, Mizoguchi returns to the theme of woman's struggle to survive intolerable conditions. Here, he offers a starkly candid view of prostitution as the epitome of the social and economic evils suffered by postwar Japan.

His "women of the night" are all victims of the war: all respectable women forced into a degrading commercial relationship with a male-dominated society that should have been the source of support and protection.

Natsuko (Sanae Takasugi, left) is reunited with her sister Fusako (Kinuyo Tanaka) in a compound for prostitutes in Women of the Night.

Fusako is a war widow. Natsuko, her younger sister, is a single woman repatriated from China. Kumiko, a sister of Fusako's husband, has lost both father and brother, and is therefore a single woman deprived of traditional male protection and authority. All three women, therefore, have in common a "single" state that means, essentially, "for sale."

Fusako's degradation is followed step by step. We first see her faithfully living up to the image of dutiful mother, daughter-in-law, and wife. She is the chief means of support for this extended family which includes her sick brother-in-law. Her earning power is confined to pawning various family possessions. When her husband, missing in action, is confirmed dead, one family tie is broken; then her child dies.

Fusako experiences a reversal of values in stages. First, released by misfortune from further obligation to her husband's family, she changes to another form of male-dependence. She starts working for Kuriyama, a black marketeer, and eventually becomes his mistress. The irony is clear: this, too, is dependence without security. Fusako sees how, given the nature of the dominating male, this must be so: she watches Kuriyama pursue, and victimize, her sister Natsuko. This leads to Fusako's complete rejection of the social norms by which she has lived. Selling herself, she believes, is the only way to become independent;

the only protest that she can make against all that male-dominated society represents.

Fusako's younger sister, Natsuko, already conditioned by the horrors of life in wartime China, suffers a much less severe conflict before defeat. Natsuko has already been victimized by men. She finds it almost natural to become a cabaret dancer, and to accept her sister's patron as her own. Yet she too has made a bad bargain. She contracts a venereal disease and is made pregnant by Kuriyama as well.

Kumiko's downfall is more direct. She is a juvenile delinquent to begin with, a typical product of the social and moral turmoil of defeated Japan. She sees revolt against conventional family restraints as a revolt against hardship too. Then, after being raped, she takes up the ancient inevitable profession: that of the streetwalker.

The film does more than depict the histories of these three victims of circumstance. Important questions of individual choice are posed as each woman seeks to rise above the cruel limits imposed by her status.

Fusako takes the lead after a time spent suffering the consequences of masculine egotism and social inequity. She regains her sense of self-worth by trying to help others regain theirs. She lectures other prostitutes on the evils of their trade. She offers to deliver her sister's baby and tries to instill in Natsuko some notion of the value of motherhood. She even rescues her sister-in-law Kumiko from a raid by rival streetwalkers and argues for a return to family as a bulwark against hostile external forces.

Even so, rescue is not in sight for any of them. It is implied that oppressed women like these cannot hope for the comforts of salvation; they can only hope to endure. Natsuko may yearn for the joys of motherhood, but in this, too, she is thwarted, since the baby is stillborn. And what can become of Kumiko? The ancient rule will still hold: once a fallen woman, always a fallen woman. Fusako, too, will fail to escape from her old trade.

Though the message of the film is starkly pessimistic, Mizoguchi's women develop as characters whose vitality offers a strong counterpoise to their predicament.

While the chief merit of *Women of the Night* lies in its enrichment of the narrative context pertaining to women's plight, the film is not devoid of some notable expressive devices. For example, using simple close-ups, Mizoguchi brings Fusako's shifting emotions to the surface in moments of crisis. In the scene immediately following her discovery of Kuriyama's involvement with her own sister, she goes to the station and stands on the platform. A shot of her crying against the wooden edge of the barrier yields to a close-up of her face, on which despair and indignation are clearly registered. The sound of an approaching train makes us uneasy. Our natural response is to feel for her and to wonder: Is she going to commit suicide, now that she has lost all means of support and her sense of self-worth?

In a work of true realism like *Sisters of the Gion* we would be left with a feeling of tragic intensity. The camera would be, as it were, more uncommitted. Yet this close-up is infused with a mellow lyricism which diffuses the tragic in a more general appeal for sympathy. This feeling continues in the following scene where we see Fusako taking the decision which allows her to continue living: she tells the proprietress of the pawnshop, who doubles as a tout for prostitutes, that she is ready to take on customers.

Perhaps the strongest bid for universal sympathy—and therefore possible sentimentality—is made in the final sequence. Here words and actions merge in a scene laden with obvious symbols. It is night in the churchyard of a bombed-out chapel. The camera takes advantage of a crater to focus an unusual shot upward at the women who seem to rule this nighttime scene. Fusako appears. The camera tracks up to, then follows her, until she comes on Kumiko being threatened as an unwelcome newcomer to this band of prostitutes.

Suddenly a high-angle shot shows Fusako pushing Kumiko to the ground, reproaching her sister-in-law for her fallen state. It is an engaging moment as Fusako is shown rising above her own desperate plight to speak for all women. Though she is nearly lynched by one band of prostitutes, she urges those present to escape the horrors of the trade while there is time. Clearly, she wants to save others though she herself is lost. A following close-up of Fusako's thickly madeup face argues for the nobility and sincerity of her cry: "One unfortunate woman like me is more than enough."

Rescued from possible injury by another band of prostitutes sympathetic toward her, Fusako escapes behind the chapel with Kumiko. Here, the camera pans up along a fresco of the madonna and child, providing a parallel that is all too obvious. Certainly the scene by itself should have been enough, controlled as it is by a gradually withdrawing, high-angled camera which shows the two women and the other prostitutes crying, with the chapel ruins and darkness looming around them.

At last, Mizoguchi's efforts paid off. *Women of the Night* was not only commercially successful but dramatically innovative as well. The social phenomena of postwar Japanese society and the degenerate aspects of eroticism were almost cruelly explored by Mizoguchi's naturalistic methods.

Mizoguchi and Yoda again worked together on his next film, *Waga Koi wa Moenu (My Love Has Been Burning*, 1949). The shooting was complicated by Mizoguchi's merciless concentration on the performance of the leading man, Ichirō Sugai. Sugai worked hard on his lines, but on the set he kept muffing them. Outraged, Mizoguchi would humiliate him in public. Despite Mizoguchi's devotion, the film was again a failure. His ideas were incompatible with those of an intellectual women's liberation advocate like the heroine, and his efforts were fruitless in a political film genre where he could not make the most use of his experiential knowledge.

Waga Koi wa Moenu (My Love Has Been Burning, 1949)

Yet this low-budget film, made in a hurry, is perhaps Mizoguchi's strongest "feminist" work. Set in the 1880s in a political climate of liberal ferment—"The Movement for Freedom and People's Rights"—this film follows the career of Eiko Kageyama, a leading feminist (modeled on an actual historical figure). As might be expected, Eiko's life charts a movement from confinement to progressive freedom. This is expressed in the traditional shift from small rural community to big city then back to the country again.

Eiko's learning experience, too, is conditioned by a series of rejections as she learns the falseness of received values. The opening sequence shows her as a teenager attending a lecture by a visiting feminist, much to the displeasure of her father and brother. Her first object lesson in female inequality comes when the family maid, Chiyo, is sold to a factory. Eiko is shocked by her parents' apparent unconcern; she wants to turn her sense of outrage to some use, but finds opportunities for feminist activism few and far between in the country.

Eiko moves, therefore, to Tokyo to join her fiancé, Hayase, a member of the newly formed Liberal Party. This, of course, turns out to be the change of one form of dependence for another. Even so, Eiko has the strength of character to force the evasive Hayase to allow her to move into his boardinghouse where she has shown up without warning. Subsequently, however, she discovers that he is a government spy, so naturally she rejects him and everything for which he stands.

Eiko's career as a political activist is vigorous and independent. She writes and edits a party newspaper, and goes on lecture tours with a party leader, Omoi. She shows the courage of her convictions throughout. When her political activities lead to a prison sentence, she is offered freedom in exchange for submission to Hayase, now a police captain, who wants to marry her. She refuses, considering his offer merely an alternative form of confinement.

After her release, Eiko decides that the best way to continue sharing Omoi's commitment to the party cause is to marry him. The outcome is ironic, because her sense of fulfillment turns out to be false. The couple

Peering through a lattice window in My Love Has Been Burning, *Eiko sees this scene of an overseer beating the girls from a local mill.*

has rescued oppressed Chiyo from a mill and given her work as a live-in maid. Then Eiko discovers that her husband, the advocate for women's rights, has been having an affair with Chiyo. Eiko must react to this piece of male hypocrisy by repudiating husband and party; she returns to the country to open a school for girls whose education will include a sense of woman's rights.

My Love Has Been Burning is in general more explicit, even more exaggerated, than Mizoguchi's other postwar depictions of the social and psychological condition of women. Yet Mizoguchi achieves this without resorting to out-of-the-way cinematic devices.

One of the most powerful scenes deals with a visit by Eiko and Omoi to a local mill where girls like Chiyo are put on hard labor and forced to please men as well. The low-key photography selects and emphasizes views of narrow confinement in this workhouse where the girls are packed like animals. Eiko studies the battered women through a lattice window; when Chiyo reaches for a lamp, we see how low the ceiling is. There is even a touch reminiscent of the usurer's cruelty to Shiraito in *White Threads of the Cascade*—here, the overseer/pimp beats girls who have been tied up and kicks Chiyo around the room.

The camera in this scene pans right to Eiko watching through the lattice window of the workhouse, then keeps moving in that direction, putting her off center as she starts moving left. Obviously, she is being given mere observer status where the misery of women like Chiyo is concerned. Toward the end of this sequence, a single close-up of Chiyo's face with a wry smile set in gloom connects the following shot of the old oil lamp to her desperate attempt to put an end to her misery by setting fire to the compound.

After this eye-opening event, Eiko's position shifts from passive sympathy to active involvement in the sufferings of oppressed women. After all, thanks to her political activism, she becomes one of them—a prisoner.

The ultimate degradation of women as actual prisoners is depicted in an episode in which Chiyo tries to bargain her way out of prison. She offers all that she has: her body. When she does so in a cell-like clinic, Mizoguchi is careful to avoid the actual scene of her humiliation. He fixes the camera on the empty bars of the clinic as the sinister laughter of the guards echoes on the sound track.

The film ends in rather melodramatic fashion, in a pointed display of women's solidarity. Eiko, who has left her husband, Omoi, is shown aboard the train headed for her home town where she intends to open a school for girls. The other passengers talk of nothing but her husband's victory in the recent elections. Chiyo, who has also just left her master, Omoi, enters the carriage and the two women meet face to face. The film ends with a medium close-up of the two women sharing Eiko's shawl.

Though the climactic moment obviously celebrates the drawing together of two women with enlarged senses of personal freedom, no clue is given to the outcome of their determination to implement their goals. We are left with questions about their future: Will Chiyo, a fallen woman once upon a time, be accepted by the conservative rural community? Will that same community tolerate Eiko who has left her successful husband to accomplish something of her own, on her own?

As before, Mizoguchi's vision of women's struggle offers no comfortable answers.

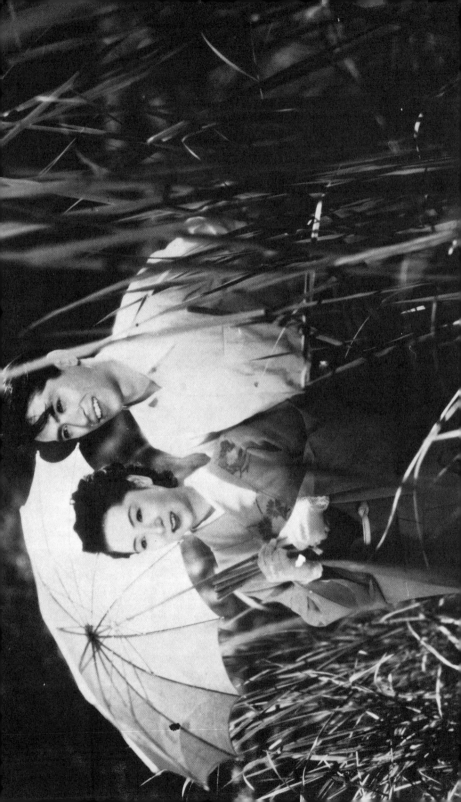

7

Rendezvous with Modern Novels:
Women of the Upper Classes (1950–51)

Another Move

AFTER MUCH negotiation and frustration connected with *Saikaku Ichidai Onna (The Life of Oharu)*, Mizoguchi resigned from the Shōchiku Company in 1950 and returned to Tokyo to work for the rival Shin Tōhō Studio. His first project there was *Yuki Fujin Ezu (A Picture of Madame Yuki*, 1950), based on the current best-seller by Seiichi Funahashi. Once again, a potentially excellent film was reduced to mediocrity by a compromise with prevailing taste. Given the mood of democratic reform in postwar Japan, Mizoguchi and his screenwriter Yoda felt reluctant to focus on a subtly erotic man/woman relationship as expressed in the attenuated values of high-minded aristocrats on the decline. Instead, they shifted the emphasis to the decidedly less interesting soul-searching of the male protagonist, a middle-class novelist (who becomes a *koto* teacher in the film). Then, too Mizoguchi's fatal egocentricity got in the way. The mood of the times was anything but favorable to his brand of studio absolutism, especially at a new company, so the films of this period show marks of strain, most notably regarding Yoda.[1]

Yuki Fujin Ezu (A Picture of Madame Yuki, 1950)

"In *A Picture of Madame Yuki* we are led to watch, with a curiosity similar to that of a voyeur, a woman torn between her unreasonable lover and her sexually appealing husband; a woman who ends by choosing death."[2] The critic Jūzaburō Futaba's comment, though sarcastic, pinpoints the basic flaw of Mizoguchi's first attempt to deal with the moral dilemma of an aristocratic woman.

The scene is set in postwar Japan, a period which saw myriad changes; among them were the abolition of class distinctions, most notably those

Lady of Musashino *(1951): Michiko (Kinuyo Tanaka) and omu (Akihiko Katayama) go for a walk on the Musashino ʾ.*

reflecting aristocratic privilege. The plot concerns the declining fortunes of Yuki, the beautiful heiress of a former count. She is unhappily married to the crude but sexually captivating Naoyuki. At the same time, she yearns to leave her practical, loose-living husband for Masaya Kikuoka, a *koto* teacher and classical example of the Platonic lover. But Masaya is too cowardly to take her away from her husband; and too unsympathetic to focus on the genuine dilemma set up by her demanding emotions which only the crude Naoyuki can satisfy. Thus the film depicts a divided Yuki playing the role of devoted wife.

Yuki's economic decline complicates the problem. When her father dies, his estate goes to pay off his and her husband's debts, so Yuki is forced to convert the family villa at Atami into an inn. First, her complete lack of skill in management shows how ill-equipped she is to free herself from the bondage of marital dependence. Then she becomes pregnant and all hope of escape seems gone.

As if that were not enough, Yuki is undone by forces beyond her control. A singer, Ayako (Naoyuki's mistress), and her manager, Tateoka, contrive to ruin Naoyuki. They not only gain control of the inn, but arrange for Naoyuki to find his innocent wife in bed with the equally innocent yet drunken Masaya. Yuki's loss of faith in both husband and lover leads her to commit suicide. Her death represents a rejection of their values, and escape from the vulgar materialism of a world where people like Tateoka and Ayako prevail.

Yuki, whose name means "snow," has all the qualities this image evokes; she is pure, sensitive, far from worldly. Yet at night she becomes the very incarnation of physical passion. The failure of this film is due in large part to miscasting. As Satō points out, the actress Michiyo Kogure cannot possibly embody a heroine like Madame Yuki.[3] She is too large, too fleshly in her tight kimono, and much too robustly energetic to appeal to our sentimental affinity for the type of remote, troubled beauty required by the role. The actress looks very much the part of a successful bourgeoise, perfectly capable of running an inn and of defending her reputation, come what may. The languishing aristocratic sufferer we need to see in Yuki is all the more noticeably absent because of the missing element of contrast required by the character of the scheming singer Ayako, who represents the successful type of postwar Japanese woman: businesslike, calculating, and uncomplicated. As it is, these two female characters *look* too much alike.

Another problem concerns Mizoguchi's treatment of Masaya, portrayed by Ken Uehara, then the best looking actor in the soft touch (*nimaime*) tradition. Too intent on not damaging the actor's image, Mizoguchi leaves him a flat character bound by a sense of noncommital righteousness. There is no dynamic display of heroism or machismo in the character of Masaya.

Despite the definite weakness in characterization, *A Picture of Madame Yuki* offers some beautifully composed scenes. Many of these make use of "flowing curtains, gauze drapery," and rippling water to suggest the ambivalent, wayward character of Madame Yuki's longings.[4] Mizoguchi combines such effects with point-of-view narrative technique to create some richly evocative visual moods.

One such scene comes at the beginning of the film. The point of reference is provided by an innocent maid, Hama, who anxiously waits for her meeting with Yuki after a separation of some years. Hama is taking a bath in the tub favored by Yuki, thinking about the beauty and elegance of the mistress she is soon to meet. The camera creates this vision for us. As if to externalize her conjecture, it moves across the clear water in the sunken tub to the water flooding out over the tile floor, then continues all the way to Yuki's room. There, it glides around the room, showing the bamboo curtain before it stops at an elaborate dressing mirror. Next, to our surprise, Hama is seen talking to a maid who tells her that the fragrance hovering around Yuki's room is from incense. The camera movement, apparently ignoring temporal continuity, adequately connects these images with the refined eroticism of the vision of Yuki which Hama forms in her mind.

In one of the climactic moments of the film, we are exposed to Yuki's sexual drive from the point of view of Hama, who is thus forced to modify her previous vision. Again the gauze curtain technique makes this possible. Hama, who has been tending to Yuki, steps out to fetch water. Suddenly Naoyuki enters and takes possession of his wife. One shot of him drawing the curtain yields to another of the curtain itself soundlessly dominating the screen. A cut to a butterfly fluttering around a stone lantern in the garden suggests a parallel to Yuki's sexual desire. Hama opens the door; a close-up shows her covering her face with her hands. Next, we see a clear contrast between light and darkness enhanced by the drawn curtain. The husband's silhouette looms behind the curtain while Hama remains in the dark outside. Naoyuki orders Hama to fold Yuki's kimono scattered around the room. Suddenly, the camera pans down and glides along the quilt barely visible through the curtain.

Though we do not see Yuki under the quilt, the slightly wavering white curtain, which resembles her skin, speaks for her; we sense her palpitating body being sexually transformed. Two close-ups (point-of-view shots) show her sash band with a buckle design of a smiling face. It is lying on the floor. The sash band is the first thing that a Japanese woman takes off in a sexual encounter. Here, it signifies Yuki's easy yielding to fleshly desire, just as the smiling face points to Hama's recognition of the other side of Yuki, as if it were deriding or destroying the maid's idealistic image of her mistress.

The final sequence constitutes perhaps the most impressive statement of Mizoguchi's aesthetics in this film. Before this, he has presented
obvious signs of Yuki's final choice of action: suicide. The kimono she
wore when she was caught with Masaya in bed has been shown scattered
around her room. Hama and her husband have been shown frantically
searching for her. Thus, when the final sequence opens with a close-up
of Yuki's tense expression as she walks along near Lake Ashi, we are
confirmed in our expectations. Furthermore, she has a Sunday kimono
on, as if she were headed for "a better journey." A series of dolly shots
follows her movement through tall grass and bushes along the shore of
the lake. The pulsating mist—another configuration of the moving gauze
curtain—half absorbs a tiny figure of Yuki, as if to prefigure her coming
death. Here there is neither sentimentality nor pathos; the camera looks
like the eye of the painter observing the contours of woman and scenery
from a distance.

Yuki finally reaches the garden of the Western-style hotel where
Masaya is staying. A series of long shots emphasizes her alienation as she
moves from the upper left of the screen to the center to sit on a wooden
chair. A waiter goes inside to get a cup of tea. There is a cut to the
interior. When the camera cuts back to the garden as the waiter returns,
Yuki is gone. At this moment, we encounter Mizoguchi's subtle manipulation of our perspective. Suddenly, he cranes the camera to the same
level with the roof of the hotel as if he were commanding us to stand on
tiptoe and look for Yuki who has disappeared through the mist toward
the lake.

The final coda once more affirms our conjecture about Yuki's destiny.
A high angle shot shows Hama crying against a tall tree near the lake.
The lake dominates the entire screen, asserting its vastness. Her cry
echoes through the morning mist hovering over the water: "Lady Yuki,
you were a coward!" Hama flings away the sash she has found lying in the
path—the same that has come to represent the latent sensuality of her
mistress. As the film ends, the camera moves out over the ripples on the
lake.

As so often, Mizoguchi loads this final shot with significance. The
image of rippling water in its natural and transferred forms has been
used throughout the film to suggest aspects of Yuki's character. Hitherto,
each image has illuminated only a part of her nature as it is perceived by
others who are ill-prepared to understand such a complex woman in
toto. All these previous water images come together in this final shot to
offer an epitome of Yuki. Thus, in the clear water of the bath we, like
Hama, have seen her innocence uncontaminated by worldly knowledge.
Then again, through the fluttering translucent curtain we have caught a
glimpse of her carnality. As Naoyuki made his way to Yuki's room to spy

on her, his dark silhouette invaded the shallow of the pond, a clear suggestion of her secret love for another man. Now at the last, the deep lake ripples and seems alive after it has engulfed and hidden in its depths all these aspects—good and bad—of Yuki, along with her body.

After *A Picture of Madame Yuki*, Mizoguchi had another reason to avoid failure. His rival Ozu, working for his former company (Shōchiku), had made *Bakushū (Early Summer)*, a film ranked best of the year in 1950. Thus Mizoguchi set out to vie with him in *Oyūsama (Miss Oyū*, released by Daiei in 1951), a film adaptation of Junichirō Tanizaki's novella, *Ashikari (The Reaper of Rushes)*.

Oyūsama (Miss Oyū, 1951)

Even though, strictly speaking, the critic must insist on the autonomy of the film at hand, there is much to learn from Mizoguchi's use of Tanizaki's novella, *The Reaper of Rushes*.

Miss Oyū, in both the original and the film, is a modern-day prototype of a Heian lady: a woman of the higher class, beautiful, elegant, and accomplished. As if he were enticing us to look for the court lady behind the ancient gauze curtain *(michō)*, the novelist Tanizaki makes us glimpse her through many layers of narrative eyes: the narrator-traveler who watches at a distance while a *koto* recital is being held at a mansion in the countryside; another equally distant observer-traveler who tells the narrator the story of Oyū; and this interior narrator's own father whose account of Oyū he (the interior narrator) remembers being told in his childhood.[5]

Mizoguchi discards this complex narrative layering in order to present a straightforward account of Shinnosuke's infatuation with Oyū. Thus our access to the "mystery" of this woman is largely confined to a single character's awareness of, and contact with, her. Of course, Mizoguchi also marshals surrounding effects, enriching our vision of Miss Oyū through carefully selected props, exquisite sets designed by Hiroshi Mizutani, and the sensitively mobile camera work of Kazuo Miyagawa.

Thus the film presents a history of unhappy love: how Shinnosuke's life is shaped by his unquenchable passion for Miss Oyū. Both belong to a social class whose ruling passion is propriety. Thus Shinnosuke would propose marriage if he could, but he cannot. To do so would constitute an unthinkable breach of decorum, since Oyū is widowed with a son and, therefore, still tied to her late husband's family. Shinnosuke must choose between marrying someone else, or remaining single—a victim of an impossible dream. He does try to balance the conflicting values. He marries Oyū's sister, Oshizu. She is sympathetic to Shinnosuke's true feelings and volunteers to be his wife in name only, and thus give him access to Oyū (suitably chaperoned, of course, by Oshizu).

Even this compromise with happiness is foredoomed to fail. Rumors of a triangular relationship spring up and create a scandal. Then Oyū's son dies, forcing her departure from her late husband's household and all its luxury, and her subsequent marriage to an affluent sake-brewer. Oyū's plea to Shinnosuke to make her younger sister a real wife, together with his financial decline, induces him to move to Tokyo away from Oyū at Fushimi in Kyoto. This separation takes us to the last stage of Shinnosuke's doomed love: final separation from his loved ones. Oshizu dies in childbirth, so Shinnosuke leaves the baby at Oyū's house and wanders off to vanish in a marsh.

Each stage of Shinnosuke's awareness of Oyū is presented in the atmosphere of the *fūga*, or elegant aestheticism cultivated as the ethos of Heian courtly life. His first two encounters with her take place on highly formal occasions in that milieu. The first is a tea ceremony held outdoors on the occasion of Shinnosuke's arranged meeting with his prospective bride, Oshizu.

The camera work here makes use of lateral and diagonal panning in combination with the long shot. The effect is one of a scroll painting opening steadily, so that we expect all that lies in the individual character's line of sight to unfold before us in due time. Thus we first see Shinnosuke coming out of the house and passing along the wall to the garden to look around. The camera follows him, adopting his perspective, traveling diagonally along the bamboo bushes, then across to the empty tea house. Finally, we see what he expects to see: the approaching party made up of Oshizu, Oyū, and others.

Even as Shinnosuke bows to them, the versatile camera, with almost floating liquidity, counterpoints the firm, unfleeting impression of the beautiful Oyū on him. Even though their encounter consists of a short moment required for bowing, it is enough. During this instant, he falls in love with Oyū, thinking that she is his bride-to-be.

A touch of delicate refinement, established earlier by a singing nightingale and the vast, well-tended garden, is reinforced by the actual scene of tea ceremony. The effect this time is created by drawing the camera back and forth. An extreme long shot of the party occupying a tiny portion of the lower left of the screen makes the blossoming cherry trees and the huge umbrella (under which the tea ceremony is held) seem very imposing. Who would suspect that this peaceful and elegant atmosphere contains in itself an element of fatal discord? The camera gradually tracks up to show the party under the umbrella in a long-medium shot.

Here, insistence on long shots clearly emphasizes the blend of individual characters and setting. It is also expressive of the atmosphere:

In Miss Oyū, *Shinnosuke (Yūji Hori, second from left), falls in
love with Oyū (Kinuyo Tanaka, second from right) during the
tea ceremony arranged to introduce him to his prospective bride
Oshizu (Nobuko Otowa, extreme right).*

Shinnosuke in the presence of someone he cannot yet capture as a real
human being. Oyū is never sought out in close-up; only Oshizu is
presented this way, so that we witness her bewildered sensitivity to
Shinnosuke's feelings for her sister as an element at odds with the
serenity of the occasion.

Mizoguchi adopts a different technique for Shinnosuke's second encounter with Oyū. This time, she is performing for the public in a *koto*
recital. Here, the mood of adoration is general: the camera cross-cuts
between members of the audience to show their adoring appreciation of
Oyū's beauty and talent. At the same time, her enigmatic remoteness is
presented through Shinnosuke by indirection; his every view (with one
exception) shows her from behind the classic bamboo blind. Thus, the
lover's fantasy is served; we see Oyū reformed in Shinnosuke's mind.
She becomes that elegant Heian lady. She is even dressed for the part,
with her long hair reaching down to the middle of her back. Other cues,
too, are provided. The camera cuts to a vase, calligraphy set, and incense
burner, all symbols of courtly high culture—all impressing on us the
actuality of convergence of past and present taking place in Shinnosuke's
mind as he forms his image of the ideal woman around Miss Oyū.

Thus the first two encounters set the scene for Shinnosuke's first moral crisis, when he must decide his future. The moment of decision comes when Shinnosuke, finding Oyū become suddenly ill on the road, guides her to the house of an acquaintance so that she can rest. As in the first incident, Mizoguchi takes advantage of the openness typical of Japanese architecture: the camera moves along freely with the couple as they enter a gate, cross a courtyard, and pass down a corridor into the room where Oyū lies down. Naturally, the camera's mobility has fully exposed the structured interior of an elegant teahouselike building appropriate for an upper-class people's tryst.

First the proprietress tends to Oyū; then a doctor is called in. Finally, Shinnosuke sits alone by the quilt bed aligned diagonally across the screen. The composition here recalls the scene of Kikunosuke attending Otoku's deathbed in *The Story of the Last Chrysanthemum*. The sinister string music on the sound track is also reminiscent of the accompaniment of Princess Wakasa's seduction of the potter in *Ugetsu*. The suggestion here is that Shinnosuke is torn between embracing Oyū and leaving her and her nobility untouched. The camera hovers almost still, moving just slightly closer to Shinnosuke to show his wavering emotions more clearly. He lights a cigarette, but in vain; then the camera moves to the left with him as he prepares to embrace Oyū—only to meet her opening eyes at this inopportune moment.

During this crisis, together with Shinnosuke, we gain a clearer vision of Oyū. Here, she is not seen in association with symbols of high culture such as the incense burner, the bamboo curtain, and the *koto*. Oyū becomes more communicative than before. She asks Shinnosuke to marry Oshizu. At one point during their confrontation, Mizoguchi cuts to Oyū in close-up in order to contrast her innocence and indifference with Shinnosuke's suppressed passion and frustration.

Significantly, here we also gain great insight into a typical Mizoguchi prototype—the unassertive, vacillating male. Shinnosuke hesitates so much as to be unable to force himself on Oyū, and thus misses the only such chance in his life. When begged by Oyū to take her sister for his wife, he cannot express himself except in a weak, affirmative tone. Mizoguchi uses a long take to underscore Shinnosuke's malingering attitude. Here again, Japanese domestic arrangements allow a more versatile following of a character's movement. Shinnosuke moves away from Oyū's room toward the partition which opens onto the courtyard occupying the upper right of the screen. He sits down. Then Oyū joins him. A ninety-degree pan suddenly follows, showing us Shinnosuke's back as he feebly agrees to Oyū's request. Thus this last shot literally represents his inability to face Oyū with a declaration of his true feelings.

Shinnosuke's fourth contact with Oyū is through Oshizu. She is his bride now. On her wedding night, knowing of his deep love of Oyū, she pleaded with him to consider her in the light of a devoted sister, not a wife. Again, this encounter is enveloped in an atmosphere of leisurely aestheticism. The three of them walk along paths in a verdant grove with blooming peonies. They emerge from a pleasure boat reminiscent of those used by the Heian aristocracy. Despite the seemingly idyllic atmosphere, this scene is full of hints of emotional crises to which Oyū is apparently blind. Her naiveté, innocence, and obliviousness are reflected in the shifting emotions of the newlyweds. Mizoguchi repeatedly cuts to Oshizu in close-up in order to register her quandary, as at the moment when the proprietress of an inn mistakes Oyū for Shinnosuke's wife. In a shot reminiscent of a similar moment showing Madame Yuki near Lake Ashi, Mizoguchi shows the forlorn Oshizu in an extreme long shot gazing at a pond after she has left Oyū and her husband alone at the inn.

This incident connects with Oyū's belated realization that she is the cause of the couple's misery. This takes place on their last pleasure trip together. Here, Oyu's nature is revealed more directly, not through the medium of associative imagery. As in the wedding night scene, Mizoguchi presents this final confrontation of the three in a long take. Spatial movement is provided by a slight lateral panning and figures moving out of frame. The camera shows all three; then Oshizu moves out of frame as Oyū approaches Shinnosuke standing near a pillar. She asks him to be her sister's real husband, declaring that unless he does so, she will no longer consider Oshizu to be her sister. Then she leaves. The camera moves left to show Oshizu alone.

This long take yields to an extremely long, high-angle shot of Shinnosuke on the beach. This effect intensifies our sense of his inability to control his fate. While the camera gradually tracks up to him, we hear the whine of a departing ship; this mournful echo suggests the aching emptiness left in his heart by Oyū's final departure from his life. Shinnosuke has been abandoned by his surrogate wife. As we expect, the next scene shows a maid telling Shinnosuke and Oshizu that Oyū has already gone.

The final sequence is the most intense. It unfolds the drama of Shinnosuke's final approach to Oyū. Here, denied access to her, he leaves his and Oshizu's infant in the garden of Oyū's country villa. Thus his child becomes the sole contact between the two. A flowing traveling shot opens this section, showing the extent of luxury and good taste lavished on the villa facing the pond. The alert viewer will recognize the building as one reminiscent of the *shinden* style (used for the residence of Heian court nobles). The occasion is a traditional moon viewing festival. Oyū is to give a *koto* recital. Here, she is most thoroughly presented in Heian atmosphere. She is dressed like a court lady in formal attire; the camera carefully travels the length of her elaborate *koto*. A series of continuous long shots seems to stress the idea that Oyū is completely at one with these lyrical surroundings. (The long shot also turns out to be a convenient method for shooting the middle-aged actress Kinuyo Tanaka cast as the twenty-year-old Oyū.) Yet here, too, a note of disharmony creeps in. All is not well with Oyū. The subsequent dialogue, along with earlier events, reveals that she is cut off from human affection: her brother has married her off for money and family prestige; her sake-brewer husband is a philanderer; Oshizu, once her closest friend, is now dead in childbirth; and now, unbeknown to her, Shinnosuke is nearing death. Thus, Oyū's pursuit of aesthetic pleasure is simply a means of escape from her solitary existence.

A maid discovers the baby in the garden, and brings it in, with a letter from Shinnosuke in which he asks Oyū to take care of the child. Significantly, the baby, the offspring of the fatal union between the doomed couple, will replace the son Oyū has lost, and will restore meaning and energy to her life. It will also be her means of reviving the past in the present and connecting both with the future. Oyū, celebrating the arrival of the new infant, asks her *koto* teacher to play.

This takes us to a final coda expressive of the evanescence of love. The familiar images of hazy moon and flow of marsh water, quite plainly reinforce this theme, along with the song from a Noh play which Shinnosuke sings:

> Without you here
> Everytime I think upon it
> All seems melancholy.
> Osaka and my life
> All the more unbearable.
> Don't think badly of me;
> Our love was ill-fated.

Interestingly enough, Mizoguchi overworks the stylistics of a fairly simple subject—the pathos of unrequited love. Sinister music accompanies an extreme long shot of a boat with two men in it gliding quietly (screen left) across the marsh. A medium shot of a man getting out of the boat tells us that one of them is Shinnosuke. He walks among the rushes like a Noh actor playing the ghost, singing the above song. The ghostly moon and the tall rushes he disappears behind evoke an eerie atmosphere, reminding us of the *shinpa* stage setting.

However, the mood created here is dispassionate rather than melodramatic, since Shinnosuke remains isolated from these surroundings. Nature here remains indifferent to the human predicament. This impression strengthens our sense of Shinnosuke's dejected isolation. We do feel the pathos of his situation; all that has gone before has prepared us to understand his reasons for losing himself in the moonlit marsh. Moreover, the officiously careful rhythm of the camera work suggests that this man's journey is tending toward heaven itself. This is in striking contrast to the earlier, more hesitant camera panning up over a hedge to reveal Oshizu and Shinnosuke's destitute little house. Similarly, the song sung by Shinnosuke in the marsh connects with the earlier happy, yet fateful outing when he and Oyū sang the same tune in a duet. As so often with Mizoguchi, the coda sounds a note of pathos that convinces and connects the viewer with the film, because he has managed to make sense of images so masterfully expressive of the tragic human condition.

Sensitive, as always, to feminine beauty, Mizoguchi could have done better in portraying the elegant upper-class life of Miss Oyū. However, his paradoxical personality again stood in the way of a genuine display of his talent as a director. He was forever vacillating between conflicting views of the film as pure art and as entertainment.

According to Yoda, there was more idiosyncratic obstinacy than troubled artistic theory in this conflict.[6] For example, he tells how Mizoguchi angrily rejected his suggestion that the rape in *A Picture of Madame Yuki* be used as a high point in the plot of the screenplay. That, the director said, would be to confuse the essentially "popular" art of the film with pure literature; and yet when the screenplay arrived, duly written up with the cinema public in mind, Mizoguchi rejected it, saying that it contained too many elements of popular art.

Despite his involvement with Tanizaki's work, Mizoguchi was not satisfied with *Miss Oyū.* One good outcome, however, was his partnership with Kazuo Miyagawa, whose camera style was to contribute greatly to the success of later works such as *Ugetsu* and *The Crucified Lovers.*

Mizoguchi was understandably anxious to escape creative depression. Finally, he found what he thought would do the trick: Shōhei Ōoka's best-seller *Musashino Fujin (The Lady of Musashino).* Again, he was mistaken. Ōoka, one of the leading literary lights of postwar Japan, was too much of a detached Stendhalian observer of human psychology; his milieu was too far removed from the sensual, down-to-earth world of fallen women, among whom Mizoguchi found his best subjects. For this reason, *The Lady of Musashino* (1951, produced by Tōhō), like his previous two films of 1950 and 1951, failed to rise above the commonplace.

Musashino Fujin (*The Lady of Musashino*, 1951)

The heroine in this film may be uncharacteristically upper-class, but she is betrayed and destroyed by the familiar hostile environment

Mizoguchi's women struggle (and so often fail) to survive in. Adultery is the issue here, since the film is set in the heady democratic climate of postwar Japan, a time when a number of such crimes were taken out of the statutes, along with their feudal penalties.

The heroine, Michiko, represents traditional morality. She clings to the image of the chaste wife and is betrayed and exploited by those whose steady, cynical gaze is fixed on the money value of everything, especially sex.

Tomiko, the antiheroine, is married to Michiko's cousin, Ōno. When he runs into serious financial trouble, she prepares to look for security elsewhere. Her husband is not offended by her obvious coquettishness; it flatters his sense of possession. However, when the moment of crisis comes, he proves extremely jealous.

Tomiko's eye falls on Michiko's husband, Akiyama. He yields to her blandishments with a readiness appropriate (so he thinks) to a Stendhalian scholar like himself. To him, adultery signifies stimulus. However, it leads him to promise Tomiko that he will marry her if he can succeed in getting hold of his wife's property. Michiko's property is also coveted by Ōno, who wants her to let him use it as surety for a loan. Thus Michiko is surrounded by those who consider themselves better fit, by virtue of the modern age, to take control of her life.

The single exception is another cousin, Tsutomu. He is a rootless man, a repatriate from wartime Burma. Both old and new value systems conflict in him. He is deeply in love with Michiko, yet he trades this exalted, Platonic attachment for an inconsequential fling with Tomiko. Even so, at the time of Michiko's death, he values her memory more than the property she has left him.

The Lady of Musashino is a good example of a film whose screenplay is impoverished by a too rigid moral scheme. The characters come to represent moral positions more than actual human beings. The novelist Ōoka avoids this danger in his book by using expressive devices, for example, eye imagery, which Mizoguchi might well have taken advantage of. Instead, he sacrifices subtle psychology to a kind of often merely verbal confrontation. The result is a film whose characters exhibit fewer shifts of position than the screenplay requires, with the result that the viewer's responses are correspondingly oversimplified and therefore less interesting than they might have been.

Despite these disappointing aspects, *The Lady of Musashino* provides some instances of Mizoguchi's fine power of observation in nature. One such example is the opening scene. Using the constantly moving camera and various shot-sizes and angles, Mizoguchi shows us individual parts of the mise-en-scène—tall trees, streams, narrow paths and the old hedge of Michiko's house—in a way that brings the Musashino

Plain to life. Similarly, as Michiko and Tsutomu walk through this landscape, Mizoguchi's pervasive long shots emphasize the sense of harmony with the best of their environment. Michiko's white parasol, for example, suggests the image of her as a tiny flower blooming in the wilderness.

Like *A Picture of Madame Yuki*, this film ends with the inevitable sense of entrapment clearly demonstrated by the heroine's suicide. As in the final coda, with its close-up of the dead heroine's face in *The Love of Sumako the Actress*, a rare close-up of Michiko's face at the moment of her death is wasted because the film's action itself has already convincingly finalized the betrayal of innocence.

Tsutomu has abandoned the right of inheritance to Michiko's property designated in her will. The traveling camera, using his line of sight, surveys the ugliness of downtown Tokyo, which will soon reach out and blemish the Musashino Plain. What is Tsutomu going to do? The plain has been the proving ground for his sense of himself and the world; he has learned the importance of human trust and also its frailty. It is after all Tsutomu who broke the lovers' vow that he and Michiko should be faithful to each other. Will Tsutomu build a new life on that failure? The ending gives no clue.

Again, each of these three films offers only small satisfactions, yet each rewards a critical examination with insights into Mizoguchi's art.

11.

8

International Attention:
Two Classics Recognized (1952–53)

Success at Last

AFTER SO many attempts, Mizoguchi broke out of his postwar dol-drums in 1952 with one of his very finest films, *Saikaku Ichidai Onna* (*The Life of Oharu*), based on the seventeenth-century classic novel by Saikaku Ihara. The making of this film had much in common with its ill-fated predecessors. Again, Mizoguchi's determination to achieve a masterpiece brought out his demonic side. Nothing less than absolute perfection would do, no matter how many retakes had to be made, no matter how often actors were put through their paces. In spite of a supposedly strictly controlled budget, nothing but the finest in the way of sets and props would do. This film was to be shot "under the best available conditions."

One of the most interesting aspects of Mizoguchi's art was his reliance on improvisation. He never bothered to work out the contents of a given scene in detail beforehand, but followed his bent as the spirit moved him. Time and again he arrived on the set where, presumably, all was in readiness for the day's work—then the director would order any number of changes. And once such changes were put in effect, they might well be changed again and again. At least one assistant director walked out on the filming of *The Life of Oharu*.

Even so, Japanese critics instantly recognized it as a masterpiece. Japanese audiences, however, were much less enthusiastic, and the film was a commercial disaster. Nevertheless, failure at home was sweetened by success abroad: *The Life of Oharu* brought Mizoguchi into the international limelight when he shared the best director award (the Silver Lion) with John Ford (for *The Quiet Man*) at the 1952 Venice Festival.

Another masterpiece followed in 1953, when Mizoguchi made *Ugetsu Monogatari* (*Ugetsu*). The script this time was based on two short stories from a nineteenth-century collection of gothic fiction, Akinari Ueda's

e Life of Oharu: *Oharu (Kinuyo Tanaka) fails to kill herself
er her lover's execution.*

Ugetsu Monogatari (Tales of Moonlight and Rain). As before, Mizoguchi's exacting artistic standards brought out the tyrant in him. This time, his longtime long-suffering scriptwriter, Yoda, revised scenes over and over again as actors were subjected to repeated retakes.

Once again, demonic persistence paid off. *Ugetsu* was shown at the Venice Festival in 1953, this time with Mizoguchi in attendance. It was his first trip abroad. Rumor had it that *Ugetsu* was in the running for a Silver Lion nomination, along with William Wyler's *Roman Holiday*. Mizoguchi confined himself to his hotel, praying to a scroll portrait of Saint Nichiren tacked to the wall. Under these difficult circumstances he was introduced to Wyler, whom he met with a face set in stern enmity. Mizoguchi won over Wyler: he won a Silver Lion and also the Italian Critics' Award.

Mizoguchi's first experience of a wide screen/70mm. film in Venice brought out his streak of eccentric violence. He was so astonished, so shocked, that he pressed his head against a wall and smacked it resoundingly with his hands. Shindō claims that Mizoguchi had every intention of setting up such a wide screen on the gigantic front gate of Chionin Temple (the largest wooden gate in Kyoto) by way of revolutionizing Japanese filmmaking.[1]

That idea, like so many others equally grandiose, equally "Mizoguchi," was never put into effect. *Ugetsu* was to be his final masterpiece. As a figure to be reckoned with on the international film scene, he had just three years to live.

Saikaku Ichidai Onna (The Life of Oharu, 1952)

In *The Life of Oharu*, Mizoguchi triumphantly returns to his most congenial subject matter: the fate of woman held captive by feudal values. As one might expect, he alters the seventeenth-century classic by Saikaku, *Kōshoku Ichidai Onna (The Woman Who Loved Love)*, to suit himself. In the original, Oharu is destroyed from within by her love of sex. Mizoguchi's heroine, in contrast, is ruined by forces largely beyond her control. Certainly, her first and fatal error is loving a man beneath her in rank; but after her fate is set that way in motion, she is progressively degraded by the customs and standards of Japanese feudal society.[2] Like so many other Mizoguchi heroines, however, she falls nobly, retaining her original dignity and integrity.

Thus Oharu joins the pathetic tragic heroines of *Osaka Elegy* and *Sisters of the Gion*. However, what makes *The Life of Oharu* and the subsequent *Ugetsu* rise above those prewar masterpieces is an enrichment of the expressive modes which also elicit richer responses to each film's thematic progression, including a greater cathartic effect.

Stylistic rigor is a term one might use to describe the pictorial quality of *The Life of Oharu*. This alone gives the film an outstanding merit. Mizoguchi's achievement here is made through the famous one-scene, one-shot method with dollying, long shots, and fairly consistently used "diagonal lines."[3] Thus we are led to "gaze" at each stage of Oharu's conflict with social forces with minds open to judgment of those social forces, and emotions engaged by their destruction of this woman.

One might add that this two-hour-and-seventeen-minute film has only 197 shots, each marked by sustained movement rather than the lengthy dialogue which got in the way in *The Loyal 47 Ronin*.

Another important gain from this rigorous control of the camera is rhetorical. Mizoguchi lets the camera do the talking in a much more subtle way than before. His style may be said to reflect the strange ambivalence of his attitude toward women; his cold, distant observation of Oharu's life is modified by warm, lyrical sympathy for her sufferings.

Discarding the orthodoxy of straightforward narrative progression, Mizoguchi renders a more striking import of Oharu's plight. The opening sequence shows her at the worst of her declining fortunes. She is a middle-aged streetwalker who can handle customers only in darkness. Here, the camera describes a consistently diagonal movement as it follows and stops with her. Except for a few instances, the camera's long look is fixed on her back. Expert as always with women's gait, Mizoguchi knows very well that a little quivering of her back and the drooping shoulderlines which her kimono emphasizes can tell us more about her state than her face: that she is cold and destitute.

The opening sequence also shows a continuing use of low-key photography and long shots. When Oharu joins the other prostitutes near the supporting pillars under the elevated floor of a temple, the fusion of this group with the dully monochromatic texture creates the desired effect of oppressive forces at work on these women. Unable to find any customers, they make this shelter their own and make a fire to warm themselves. Yet even here, society pursues these female victims with cruel indifference to their misery. The force in question here is religion. The camera pans up to show a monk on high—on the elevated floor. He tells them not to endanger the temple, as if they were the lowest of society.

Oharu's situation having been established, her recollection of the past begins. We find her inside the main hall of the temple. Low-key photography and the image of the stone floor again transmit a sense of the damp and cold which Oharu has to endure. As the camera sweeps across the statues inside the hall, for the first time we have a chance to scrutinize Oharu's face in close-up: an old, weary face coated with thick makeup. But when she mysteriously and suddenly smiles, her face does not exhibit anything like self-derision or humility, but rather has a subtle striking sparkling of refinement mixed with even a touch of dignity beneath the ugliness of age. A close-up of the face of a Buddhist statue is superimposed upon that of a young samurai. This is how the flashback begins. The solemn Noh music seems to externalize Oharu's prayer for the samurai, Katsunosuke, her first love, whose punishment for loving above his rank, was death. This is taken over by elegant court music (*gagaku*) as the flashback takes us back to some twenty years earlier when Oharu was a lady of the court.

Thus, in the flashback, the first stage of Oharu's declining fortunes is presented. As a series of long shots shows Oharu gracefully walking, followed by a young attendant and completedly attuned to the courtly atmosphere, we realize that Mizoguchi's chronological reverse serves him well in elucidating how drastically time and misfortune have transformed this woman. Here, Mizoguchi attributes Oharu's ill luck to the basic incompatibility between *giri* ("social obligation") and *ninjō* ("personal feelings"). Oharu is initially prone to accept the feudal code which prohibits her from marrying or even having an affair with Katsunosuke. But then her admirer's genuine and persistent devotion moves her to the other extreme of personal indulgence, and ultimately, defiance.

In the famous love scene, Mizoguchi employs the one-scene, one-shot method.[4] He makes such inspired use of the traditional Japanese house and garden that the location itself, along with the vertical disposition of the actors, is richly expressive of the changing emotions of the heroine. In fact, precisely because of the variables in composition allowed by the long take, we are unaware of its duration.

Thus a few opening shots yield to a long take of Katsunosuke outside confessing his love to Oharu inside the annex of a Japanese inn. One room partition is already open; Oharu opens another which separates the annex from the exterior. This allows Katsunosuke to move toward her. She is standing while he kneels. This alignment clearly shows Oharu's dignity and pride in refusing the advances of a man beneath her status when she tells him who she is. Katsunosuke says that he has lured her into the inn, sending a false letter ordering her to meet a certain court noble here. Oharu steps down to the garden and reminds him that custom forbids their even meeting.

However, from this point on, the couple's arrangement within the frame radically shifts, faithful to masculine assertiveness in man-woman relationships. Katsunosuke embraces Oharu. She runs to the site of the stupas and falls on the ground while he remains standing. He carries her into the room, leaving one stupa dominating the screen. This uninhabited landscape, which terminates the long take, constitutes a stasis. It tells us that this abortive love affair must bring death to the lovers. As we expect, Oharu and Katsunosuke are soon arrested by police officials who rush into the inn. Oharu is sent away while Katsunosuke is sentenced to death.

A similar long take which maximizes the traveling shot is employed when Oharu, reading Katsunosuke's last letter which tells her to be true to herself, rushes out from the house and runs into the bamboo grove, ready to stab herself. Her mother follows. The camera moves with Oharu, varying directions in order to express her emotional confusion. When it finally stops with her in the bamboo grove, a high-angle long shot conveys Oharu's dejection: her alienation from lover, parents, and society.

The scenes which follow the lovers' arrest contain striking moments of the expressive power of the camera. As Satō points out, one such example is found in the scene where Oharu and her parents are expelled from Kyoto.[5] The initial high-angle long shot of the party on the river bank articulates the felt life of the punished: shame, helplessness, and alienation. A low-angle shot follows as they are escorted by relatives as far as the middle of the bridge, then cross it alone to find themselves on the other side. Oharu and her parents occupy a tiny spot in the upper corner of the screen. The camera's eye is cold and distant, as if Mizoguchi were seeing these people as criminals. Suddenly, however, he moves the camera under the bridge to look up at them as if he were expressing sympathy for them as social victims. As usual, the fade, the familiar punctuation for elegizing personal plight, closes the scene.

The other scene Satō cites is the execution of Katsunosuke. There is a close-up of a sword placed diagonally across his chest by the executioner. It is held firmly, as if to suggest the *merihari* device, a sudden halt in one action leading to a sublime, decisive result in another. Next, we see a shot of the sword lifted in midair, then the camera pans with it gradually lowered to the ground. According to Satō, the camera's movement looks as if the director had lowered his head, expressing his sorrow for the unfortunate young man.[6]

Here, violence is ritually presented. There is no sound of the sword thrust back into the sheath. There are no blood stains on the sword or the sounds of its being washed clean. Utter silence prevails at this awesome moment.

The only weakness found in Mizoguchi's portrayal of Oharu's first moral conflict is that he does not dramatize her vacillation between *giri* and *ninjō* with sufficient intensity. Her shift of values is so sudden when Katsunosuke woos her that we are somewhat bewildered at the cause. This lack of evidence of conflict tends to lessen the effect of thematic and stylistic input in the scenes of Oharu's exile and her subsequent lamentation over Katsunosuke's death.

What we do understand as the film proceeds is that Oharu's giving in to forbidden love has consequences that are demonstrated with fateful clarity. We may not have experienced her initial conflict in full, but we are led to participate in the spectacle of her degradation as a woman entirely at the mercy of forces from without.

The second stage of her downward fall comes when she is merchandised—given as a concubine to the rich Lord Matsudaira. Her parents hope to profit materially from this; the Matsudaira clan expects to use her as a surrogate mother, a useful receptacle for the heir this great family needs for its continuation.

A number of visual clues are given to convey a sense of Oharu's plight. The camera in close-up captures the portrait scroll depicting the sort of ideal beauty the Matsudaira clan is desperately searching for to mate with its aging lord. The camera slowly pans down this elegant female body like some customer coolly appraising goods put up for sale. We see Oharu rushed along cramped in a palanquin en route to the Matsudaira mansion where she is confined by high folding panels, first, to be examined by a doctor and various palace beldames, then in order to give birth to the future lord and master of the place—all images of entrapment pure and simple.

Her mission accomplished, Oharu is dismissed—sent home to her parents with a miserly sum in compensation, much to her father's chagrin. Again, Mizoguchi underlines the absolute power of money and patriarchy in a woman's life, this time by showing Oharu's father selling his daughter to the Shimabara Pleasure District in order to settle some debts.

Here we see Oharu revolting against money-oriented and male-dominated society in the only way she knows: she despises the men she is supposed to please. From various angles and in various shot sizes, Oharu is shown stubbornly aloof from her unfriendly environment. While other courtesans are busy, scrambling for coins thrown on the floor by a merchant, Oharu sits immobile. The proprietor blames Oharu for being proud. More emphatically, Oharu's integrity is captured by the stable camera when she quietly, with her body upright and her eyes looking straight ahead, climbs upstairs to meet a wealthy customer, after the proprietor, now friendly, bows and pleads with her to serve him.

When the wealthy merchant, who promises to redeem her, turns out to be a counterfeiter, he is chased by police officials who corner him in the courtyard of the pleasure house. Suddenly, the camera is withdrawn to show the entire building; on the second floor, Oharu is shown in a long shot, standing upright and watching indifferently the incident, which nonetheless helps determine her fate never to escape enslavement by the forces of materialism and patriarchy.

The fourth stage of her decline after her terms of service at Shimabara takes her to the affluent merchant Kabei's house where she works as a hairdresser for his wife, who covers her bald head with a wig. Again, circumstances beyond her control—the husband's lust and the wife's jealousy—force her to leave.

The only promise of a settled, conventional, respectable life comes in the form of marriage to a fanmaker. Even here, a commercial transaction comes into it, since the prospective husband has promised his father-in-law a certain sum of money. And just as money seems to open the way to happiness, money ends it all: the fanmaker is killed by a thief on his day of collection.

The marriage sequence is brief, as befits such a modest bloom of happiness for Oharu. Two long takes say it all; and yet Mizoguchi achieves some masterful contrasts using the most sparing means. Interestingly enough, the cold detached objectivity of the camera eye yields here to a warmly subjective feeling. The one-scene, one-shot device presents Oharu, now attired in a subdued kimono, tidying the shop. She looks like a settled housewife. As usual, the spatial flow is reinforced by the characters moving in and out. Her husband appears; and Oharu sees him off. Both of them disappear behind the shop curtain hanging at the entrance, a convenient prop for compositional variation. Oharu returns to mind the store. Two customers—a mother and daughter—come in, and Oharu joyously waits on them. Some festive music, for a change, is heard on the sound track. Unlike the entrance door, the shop curtain does not cover the entire front, so we can see pedestrians from the waist down passing by in both directions while Oharu chats with the customers. The shop is in a good business district. The visual images, the dialogue, and the music all unite to make us see the felt reality of Oharu's fulfillment.

The second one-scene, one-shot method shows Oharu inside the shop alone in darkness. The music is now gone. When the police officials arrive, she greets them in front and they all enter, followed by the camera. The officials put down a wooden litter with a man's body on it. It is her husband. The camera lowers with Oharu as she kneels, as if to lead us into sympathy for her. She now bends over his body and cries, while one of the officials reports that her husband was found dead holding a sash firmly in his hand. It was the sash which he had promised Oharu.

Sensitive to a woman's posture in despair, Mizoguchi has thus far shown Oharu alone, frequently prostrate on the ground (as in the scene at the Matsudaira's mansion where her baby was taken away by his lordship's wife). By now we have been conditioned to develop an affinity for the pathos of her life through this gesture. Here Mizoguchi also works overtime to elicit our emotional response. The incantationlike sutra prayer and Oharu's cry merge. He closes the second long take with his familiar emotive punctuation: the fade.

The sixth turning point in Oharu's life is her decision to enter a nunnery. The initial shot, with a beautiful pictorial effect, visualizes her yearning for repose. Again, the sutra incantation dominates the sound track. A high-angle shot shows a nun dressed in black walking around a stone lantern placed in front of a pond. The sand in the courtyard is raked. The drizzling rain, an apt metaphor for the quiet atmosphere, provides vague, vertical lines to the screen. As the nun moves screen right, we see a part of the interior of the temple where Oharu, taken in an extreme long shot, sits quietly and humbly, occupying the upper right of the screen. This decentering of Oharu, with the courtyard dominating the screen, creates the impression that serenity is finally within her reach.

Yet this place of spiritual refuge is not proof against the outside world. Money and license come to victimize Oharu. The head clerk of Kabei's store where Oharu worked as a hairdresser comes to demand payment for the kimono material which she bought on credit from an apprentice clerk, Bunkichi, who was infatuated with her. Oharu cannot pay. All she can do is to take off the kimono which she has already made out of the material; worse yet, she is thus forced to make herself available to the head clerk.

Significantly, his actual advances take place behind a huge folding decorative screen. Throughout the second half of the film, we are denied access to actual seduction scenes. In another instance, when the merchant Kabei makes advances to Oharu, he chants a sutra, walking on his knees toward Oharu who is out of frame. As some critics point out, this device weakens the dramatic effect, because we are kept from fuller exposure to Oharu's affective life—her manner of resigning and responding to male assertiveness at moments of moral crisis.[7]

Oharu must roam the world again, having been caught in the act by the nun. The final shot of the nunnery sequence is charged with suggestions of pathos. Again, a high-angle, extremely long shot returns to show Oharu walk through the anteroom screen right, descend a few steps connected with the earthen floor, and then disappear through the exit. She looks pitifully small, diminished in physical and moral stature, a sufferer from both physical and social coldness. Her very walk conveys a sense of the forlorn. Here, as elsewhere, Mizoguchi seems to be using Oharu's exterior and posture, far more than facial expression, to register the sadness within as outside forces contrive to crush her.

Furthermore, the sharp metallic sound of the convent bell clangs in the chilly, deserted exit, as if the nun inside were beating it violently to chase evil spirits away or even banish her own suppressed sexual desires. This unusual form of farewell offers yet another index of Oharu's hostile surroundings. Here, she is denied compassion and understanding by the religion of the compassionate Buddha.

This sequence takes us to a kind of short parody of the *michiyuki*, the lovers' journey in the Bunraku or Kabuki theater. Here the journey is taken by the exiled: Oharu, and Bunkichi, the clerk also forced out of service for extending credit when he knew she could not pay. Now he is a fugitive for this and a bigger crime: embezzlement. Again Mizoguchi's powerful use of the one-scene, one-shot method returns. He packs a series of quick actions into the scene by moving characters and camera freely in an open setting: a small tea house for travelers open to the highway. Oharu and Bunkichi are sitting on a wooden bench. He stands up and moves to the back of the tea house (away from the camera) to order food. In deep focus, the camera shows him caught by his pursuers, who have been resting there. As Bunkichi is dragged out to the highway, the camera moves screen right with him. Oharu comes onto the scene to intervene, and we get only a momentary glimpse of her face in close-up as she moves diagonally toward the camera. This device is superbly expressive of her genuine sympathy for the down and out, despite the hardship of her own life.

Bunkichi is taken away by the officers who shove Oharu aside. This long take ends with an extreme long shot of Oharu trying in vain to run after Bunkichi's party while it disappears in the distance, occupying the upper central portion of the screen. This vertical movement of Oharu in midframe, because of its calculated symmetry, again enhances a sense of her alienation from the environment.

Another downfall finds her in a yet more destitute state. She is now a beggar, living on her art: singing and *samisen* playing. Throughout this sequence, Mizoguchi's camera is notably detached, following at a distance and moving up only occasionally for a medium shot. Yet, because of this distancing, he can elicit even stronger sympathy for the Oharu reduced this much. Needless to say, the contrasting expressive devices enhance this rhetorical effect. The series of high-angle long shots which opens this sequence emphasizes Oharu's relationship to her hostile environment. Again, Mizoguchi lets posture speak for the woman within. We see Oharu sitting by one of the pillars of a half-ruinous temple gate. Clearly, it is not the best place to be begging for bread; only one old couple passes by to give her money. This scene offers a deft counterpoise to an earlier one in which we see Oharu giving money to just such a beggar right after she leaves the Shimabara Pleasure District. The likeness is even more pointed; we remember that that beggar was also once a high-ranking courtesan at Shimabara.

The appeal to our sympathies is made even stronger when the mother/son reunion motif is introduced. Oharu sees the palanquin carrying her infant son, now the heir to Lord Matsudaira, richly escorted. She follows at a distance and watches the ritual offering of sweets to this little lord. Here the contrast between so simple and human a thing as giving candy to a child, and the feudal panoply surrounding it, serves once again to suggest that the world is too rigidly structured to include the likes of Oharu, and will in fact crush her if she refuses to keep a convenient distance.

This sense of victim-victimizer is reinforced by cross-cutting between mother and son. Yet Mizoguchi demonstrates the universal quality of maternal love—a human quality still intact even in the oppressive feudal structure—in the next long take, when he presents a medium shot of Oharu walking back to her half-ruined temple gate. Despite her wretched appearance, her face is almost radiant, her smile one of those rare, genuine expressions of happiness. We have seen her smiling this way at customers during her brief married life in the fanmaker's shop. It is very different from the self-depreciatory or cynical smiles offered colleagues and customers during her days at Shimabara.

The tragedy of social inequity which separates mother and son is given more powerful expression as Oharu approaches her gate. Japanese flute music is on the sound track, as if to speak her sorrow. Yet, the camera eye is again detached; instead of following her, it moves in the opposite direction, as if to regard Oharu's plight as just one aspect of human fate. Within the same long take, the camera is now pulled back to show Oharu crouching again at the gate. Again, despite the aloof camera, Oharu's tiny figure merging with the desolate atmosphere evokes a strong affinity for her predicament. The camera now focuses statically upon her, drawing our attention to her gesture, the sole movement on the screen. She plays a *samisen* whose intermittently broken tone expresses her feelings of the maternal bond suddenly broken. Then the flute music and her sobbing mix, vibrating through the cold air. The camera's long look terminates with her turning aside to lower her head. Two prostitutes find her sorrow-stricken and starving, and take her to their lodging.

This sequence closes with a stasis—the deserted temple gate. For the first time, Mizoguchi makes us see clearly the place covered with cobble stone where Oharu has been sitting. Almost like a shock, this image leads us to experience the coldness to which Oharu has been exposed, attired in a rather thin kimono. It also brings us face to face with the cold impersonal nature of a universe against which Oharu has no protection.

However, there is human warmth still left in this world among the lowliest kind of people: the middle-aged prostitutes who can beguile their customers only at the darkest of the night. Thus, the eighth stage of Oharu's downfall takes her to the very nadir: she joins the group of women who are on sale past their prime.

The harsh reality of this final stage of Oharu's degradation is presented in a splendidly imaginative episode which also combines a kind of defiant parody of itself. After a number of failed attempts to snag a customer, Oharu is accosted by a man who is not interested in a sexual encounter. He has something even more degrading in mind as he escorts her to a small shack. Here again, Mizoguchi employs the one-scene, one-shot method, relying for variety on camera and characters moving freely within the given frame.

This long take draws its unique character, however, from Mizoguchi's inspired determination to play appearances and reality off against one another. As they move into the back room of the shack, Oharu's customer tells her not to feign a young woman's voice. The camera moves with them to show a group of young pilgrims. The man holds a candle close to Oharu's face and begins preaching. He tells the faithful not to fall into the snare of sex during their holy pilgrimage, adding that the woman they see in front of them is a witch, an incarnation of evil. The superb contrast between light and darkness is breathtaking. Yet Oharu's thickly madeup face, which looms up, appears at first glance to damage this aesthetic effect. To the young men her face must seem grotesque and unappealing. However, we must see beyond what is there. Her wrinkled, white face with averted eyes taken in a medium shot is also the face of the woman who nobly and courageously accepts her fate. There is a strange mixture of the heroic and the wretched on her face, which makes her decline all the more pathetic.

For the first time ever, Oharu jingles the coins given her for her service. Many scenes have thus far shown her remaining aloof from money. It was Oharu who sat immobile while other courtesans were scrambling for coins thrown on the floor; Oharu who sadly watched her father counting the advance payment made by the Matsudaira clan for her services. Yet, the metallic sound of the coins here, and her cynical smile, clearly depict her half-mocking, half-disgusted estimation of herself as having become one of those whom she used to despise. From this point on, we receive cues to her felt life only from little gestures Oharu makes since Mizoguchi avoids a frontal shot of her most of the time. She stands up and moves to the corner of the room to put on a pair of sandals. Again her back, slightly bent, expresses a mixture of indignant self-contempt and quiescent resignation. But this posture is that of tension which is ready to yield to some decisive action. As we expect, she stands up and quickly moves to where she was and begins playing the witch for the benefit of those youngsters. This self-mockery seems the only way she can get even with those men who laugh at and look down upon her.

This scene takes us back to an earlier one in which Oharu is seen watching a prostitute accosting a customer, then disappearing with him into a nearby hut while Oharu herself goes into the temple. The element of repetition here is a clever device for leading us out of the flashback: we are now shown the inside of the main hall where Oharu, with a cynical tearful smile, is waking from her recollection of past life.

Here, Mizoguchi exhibits Oharu's pathos straightforwardly and powerfully, relying on a device that he has used infrequently: the close-up. The camera draws back and forth between close-up of temple statues and Oharu's face. The statues once more metamorphose into the faces of those who wronged her: Lord Matsudaira and the merchant Kabei. Naturally, her tears, which make the statues look hazy on the screen, crystallize her own outlook on her life. There is a certain purity and serenity in her acceptance of fate: no sign of raving at the hostile world. The second close-up of Oharu trying to stand up near the pillar elicits our complete sympathy. Then she loses consciousness.

From the straightforward descent of her fortunes, the film's narrative focus now shifts to a promise of reversal. This is done by the familiar motif of reunion. Oharu is united with her aged mother and is to be united with her child, now the new Lord Matsudaira. Accordingly, there is a complete change in filmic setting and composition, especially in the scene of her return to Lord Matsudaira's mansion. The emphasis here is on the cold formality associated with the house. A series of reverse-field shots shows Oharu, now dressed in a respectable kimono, sitting before rows of retainers, only to be reprimanded for having tarnished the reputation of the clan. The image of the palanquin is reintroduced. This time it is covered with netting to suggest Oharu's own return to the feudal confinement of respectability: she is to ride in it like a prisoner.

Oharu consents to this oppressive rescue only because she has hopes of being with her son. She is soon disappointed. She cannot be received, even in formal audience. Again, the conflict between simple human nature and inflexible systems costs Oharu dearly. When she is favored with a secret view of her son, from a safe distance in the corner of the garden, she revolts in the only way she knows. A lateral dolly follows as she strikes out across the garden to get a closer look at the new Lord Matsudaira. Still, she follows. The son passes her by, looking straight ahead. The final shot with deep focus and a stable camera shows the conflict resolving itself in turmoil. Retainers come forward to stop her; Oharu tells them that they are talking to the mother of their lord. There is striking dignity about her, which makes the retainers momentarily freeze in the sitting position. This is a kind of *merihari* device, which leads to an emotionally captivating action. Oharu runs and goes inside the entrance which occupies the upper right of the screen. The retainers, taken aback, run after her, and she is dragged back all the way to where she was: to the lower left of the screen. The *koto* music which opened this scene increases in volume as if to highlight Oharu's loss of her only chance of salvation in the secular world: affirmation of maternal love. The music continues even as the scene fades out, as if it were Oharu's or Mizoguchi's own sobbing.

The final coda shows Mizoguchi's return to his familiar ground: the one-scene, one-shot method. The ending not only provides us with multiple levels of experience—aesthetic, religious, and social, but also brings the film's complex issues to a final resolution. It is dusk. Two small houses stand by the roadside. The light coming through the (paper) sliding doors of the houses merges with the prevailing darkness, creating an exquisitely pictorial composition.

Oharu comes in. She is now a pilgrim in a black kimono and traveling hat. She has escaped her life as a virtual prisoner in Lord Matsudaira's mansion. Here, the theme of roaming is presented on another level. Having been denied humanistic fulfillment in the secular world, she finds it in a life devoted to *kannon*, the goddess of mercy. However, Oharu must achieve salvation through her own efforts, not as a dependent of organized religion as symbolized by the nunnery. Oharu begs alms at one house where a woman refuses her courteously. At another house, a man rudely chases her away. The message seems obvious.

As Oharu walks toward the camera, the sound track, arranged for a Western orchestra, chants the famous sutra whose text is entirely appropriate: "May my wishes be granted through the mercy of *kannon!*" The camera moves onto a pagoda in the distance as Oharu prays toward it. Here again, compositional symmetry is created by the shape shared by Oharu's traveling hat and the pagoda roof.[8] What does her prayer itself indicate? We understand that Oharu has achieved a kind of integration after all. She is last seen reaching out to the Buddhist ideal of all-embracing compassion, transcending the quest for individual salvation by means of an all-inclusive prayer for mercy. Oharu's prayer includes the lover who died on her account, and all those who caused her misfortunes as well. In this final instance, we see Oharu rising above the other Mizoguchi heroines, and becoming the best, the most sublime type of the woman who can *forgive*, even in the midst of personal misery.

As Oharu disappears, the final shot is a stasis again. The soaring pagoda, unlike the earlier stupa suggestive of death, stands in the center. The chorus repeats the sutra in a crescendo: "May my wishes be grated through the mercy of *kannon!*" It serves as a point of recapitulation of all the courses of Oharu's downfall and search for repose. The Buddhist statues which Oharu viewed twice before and after her recollection must be connected with this final coda. These statues are related to *muenbutsu*, the buddhas that the courtesans at Yoshiwara are supposed to become after their death. Certainly there is a streak of hope as the spiral of the pagoda pointing to heaven signifies Oharu's struggle or aspiration for enlightenment. Furthermore, the Japanese audience understands immediately that this ancient pagoda, which has been intact for many years, relates to the Buddhist theme of mutability, the idea that the rise and fall of an individual human's fortunes comes to seem very insignificant in the light of centuries.

Ugetsu Monogatari (Ugetsu, 1953)

Ugetsu, like Mizoguchi's other masterpieces, gives us once more a study in confrontation: the woman pitted against a man's world. Yet Ugetsu takes its place with The Life of Oharu as one of Mizoguchi's two best films, because it lifts his social concerns to a more universal plane, and does so brilliantly.

In this film the question of social restrictiveness and injustice is related to the suffering masses and to their struggle to survive the forces of oppression, even in wartime. Mizoguchi wrote about his intentions in a letter to his scriptwriter, Yoshikata Yoda: "Whether war originates in the ruler's personal motives, or in some public concern, how violence, disguised as war, oppresses and torments the populace both physically and spiritually! . . . I want to emphasize this as the main theme of the film. . . ."[9]

Such a theme might be expected to yield a highly realistic, politically committed, documentary film, yet Mizoguchi does something different. He engages with his material on several levels of perception—realistic, aesthetic, religious, and mystical—in a uniquely successful integration of theme and style.

To begin with, there are two "realities" made use of in Ugetsu: the natural world, most tangibly present in a world at war; and the supernatural of ghosts and apparitions. This duality also calls forth a range of expressive devices in similar contrast, moving back and forth between crude realism and highly stylized lyricism. Some of the resulting scenes could stand by themselves as proof of Mizoguchi's mastery in this difficult art of shifting and intersecting perspectives.

As always, Mizoguchi is at his richest and best on familiar ground: the one-scene, one-shot method; the long shot; panning; dissolve; and low-key photography generally. To those might be added a felicity of camera movement, a fluid glide from one segment to the next, resulting in a pleasing control of the total effects of pictorial composition.

The film's action concerns two ways of confronting the Japanese civil wars of the sixteenth century. The first, represented by Genjūrō, Tōbei, and, to a certain extent, Ohama, Tōbei's wife, is the way of opportunistic greed that involves geographic mobility. The second, represented by

Miyagi, Genjūrō's wife, is the way of optimistic endurance that entails devotion to community and orientation toward the future. Given the rigid societal structure of feudal Japan, where geographic mobility was not allowed to the commoner, the first way would seem inaccessible, but the turmoil of civil war that shook the foundation of feudalism itself provided enough dislocation to make it available.

The first part of the film focuses on the clash of these opposing values and the resultant dissolution of the family, while the second half shows Genjūrō's obsession with illusion and the restoration of the family.

The opening shot gives proof of Mizoguchi's mastery of camera work. Moving slowly from the general to the particular, the camera captures an entire small community at the foot of the mountain. Then, as if leading us into the world of scroll painting, it travels across a field, past a stand of trees, pans 360 degrees, and finally comes to rest on a potter and his wife in front of their small house.[10] Here is a fine transition from stillness/serenity to disorder/movement. While they are loading pottery onto a wagon, sharp reports of rifles suddenly disturb the quiet atmosphere of the village.

Throughout the first half of the film, Mizoguchi portrays the collective misery that war has brought to the villagers, by creating the appropriate mood through the combination of low-key photography and many long and medium shots. For example, only the entrances of the houses in the village are illuminated, while all else—the rest of the houses and the street—is dim. Against this backdrop, Mizoguchi presents a series of long shots of the villagers heading for cover. By not using a close-up of a single villager, Mizoguchi can emphasize collective, not individual, fear. Furthermore, this dark texture draws us right into their environment and makes us feel their suffering as something immediate to our experience.

In another scene where Genjūrō, Miyagi, Tōbei, and Ohama are busy with pottery-making, the bright fire from the kiln is interfused with the darkness of the night surrounding the four. This monochromatic effect again involves us in the quiet yet sinister nocturnal atmosphere; we feel the threat of disturbance at any time by the arrival of soldiers. In addition, at another level, we experience a visual pleasure from the compositional harmony.

Throughout this sequence with its tense evocation of opposing choices of action, Mizoguchi introduces a close-up only once and that very deftly. While the villagers flee toward the mountain, Miyagi rushes into the house to get her boy out of bed and holds him in her arms. A sudden close-up of her face fixes Miyagi in our minds as the quintessential sufferer of wartime: the mother whose love for her family serves as a kind of standard which we use to measure the worst that can be done to outrage human feelings in time of war.

One of the great, magical moments in all film-making that would alone rank Mizoguchi with the immortals: Genjūrō (Masayuki Mori), Miyagi (Kinuyo Tanaka) with her son, and Ohama (Mitsuko Mito) in the boat scene in Ugetsu.

The famous boat scene in the first half of the film is often cited as a high point of Mizoguchi's art. It follows Genjūrō's discovery that the pottery firing in the kiln while the village was overrun has been undamaged after all. The potters load their wares into a small boat and set across a lake to the town. Both families start out on this trip: Genjūrō and his wife Miyagi and small son, along with Tōbei and his wife, Ohama. A long shot of the boat emerging from the mist approaching the camera opens the scene. This in itself engenders a supernatural mood, which is also enhanced by Ohama's monotonous singing that merges with distant drum beats. The drum is interrupted from time to time by the sound of distant guns. This reminds us of the reality of war as experienced by the passengers. The boat, turning ninety degrees, shows its side. Mizoguchi's famous one-scene, one-shot method follows, fixing our attention on the five in the boat: they and it are completely subsumed into a general texture of grey, as mist slowly erases the monochromatic contrast.

When the supernatural atmosphere wanes gradually, the film takes on a marvelously realistic dimension both visually and auditorily. The men in the boat, drinking sake, begin to speak of capitalizing on the war. In contrast, Miyagi nibbles food in silence, her face expressing sad resignation.

Suddenly the one-scene, one-shot method yields to a shifting perspective as the realistic texture recedes. The supernatural atmosphere returns again as a point-of-view shot reveals a strange boat approaching from the distance. The mist still hovers over the lake. Though Mizoguchi uses open-framing here, this dark texture creates the effect of close-framing. It steeps everything in a kind of supernatural ambiance, in which we actively experience the passengers' felt reality: a sense of approaching danger. The drum beats become louder and louder, as Ohama's singing diminishes. A long shot of the two boats almost stern to stern quietly gives way to a medium shot of both.

The passengers in the boat think that the mysterious boat is haunted by ghosts. Our expectation of the supernatural, however, is, like theirs, broken when a man in the boat explains that he has been attacked by pirates, adding that they will take everything, especially women. The transition to realism is abrupt. A swift cut to the two women's anxious faces is followed by a medium shot of all concerned gathering around the dying boatman. Here too, the drumbeats do their work: we seem to hear the very heartbeats of these terrified people in the grip of the immediacy of war.

The following scene of separation, which once more reinforces the division between opportunism and resignation, reveals Mizoguchi's rigorously objective camera, subtly modified by his lyrical bent. Initially, cross-cutting between the husband in the boat and Miyagi ashore—a standard method for rendering individual relationships—elucidates the mutual caring of husband and wife, which will soon be endangered. After another intercutting between Miyagi and the other passengers, Mizoguchi lets the camera dolly along with Miyagi as she walks along the shore to see the party off. When she stops, the camera stops too, and the camera's long look, in a long shot, falls on Miyagi still standing among the tall grass watching the boat now out of screen. Here Mizoguchi has moved his camera as if he were compassionately watching this poor woman's plight, and we feel sympathy for her. A fade—the typical Mizoguchi punctuation—follows the long shot of Miyagi, sharing a more elegiac mood appropriate to her sorrow.

Mizoguchi later presents Ohama's moral quandary in a similar fashion. Here, the way of opportunism, chosen by Ohama, is worse than fruitless. While she is looking for her husband, who has disappeared in the town to buy a set of armor, she becomes the target of some roaming samurai. Their assault on her takes place in a devastated temple. As before, Mizoguchi lets the camera do the talking. As Ohama bursts into tears, surrounded by the samurai, the camera swiftly cuts back to the outside of the temple as if it could not bear to see her raped. In turn, it presents a close-up of Ohama's discarded straw sandals to allow us to imagine what is happening inside.

From this point on, the film's action dignifies her suffering partly through the director's controlled sensitivity to her figure, especially her back. When Ohama comes out after the samurai's departure, the Noh chorus vocalizes her sorrow and indignation. Just as in Miyagi's case, the camera follows straightforwardly, taking its cues from her motions. The next is an exquisite example of what a single shot can do to elicit rich response. A low angle shot shows Ohama standing in the door of the temple; she is looking up at the sky with her back to us. Her disheveled figure fits in with the desolate surroundings: the ruined temple and the gloomy sky with a waning moon. This shot alone creates the effect of black and white ink painting, while the fusion of Ohama and her environment externalizes her emotional quandary as articulated by the Noh chorus. This typical mood helps draw us into her mind more effectively than a close-up of her face. Furthermore, the entire filmic composition, especially the low angle shot, makes it appear as though Mizoguchi were looking up at Ohama, admiring her courage to struggle through life.

The latter half of *Ugetsu* is mainly concerned with Genjūrō. His opportunistic way takes a radical turn when he moves from commonplace greed to the passion of love. Accordingly, the filmic texture shifts from matter-of-fact social realism to a supernatural lyric mood. Mizoguchi's superb integration of expressive devices into the film's thematic conflict becomes clearer.

The thematic change starts with a long shot of Princess Wakasa and her attendant leading Genjūrō into her mansion. The supernatural aura is already present: the princess's face resembles the female Noh mask; and her stride is of an unearthly lightness like that of a ghost in Noh drama. Mizoguchi employs an unusually long traveling camera to show the three going down the street, through a field and into the garden of Wakasa's mansion. The overall effect of this rhythmical flow of the camera is similar to the flow of a scroll painting as we open it.

At the mansion, Mizoguchi reinforces our sense of the supernatural again in a pictorial fashion. As Genjūrō is guided down the long corridor to a back room, there is slow cross-cutting between his room and the others along the way. Darkness prevails, then yields to a soft illumination as Wakasa's servants light candles in the open rooms. The timing for this textural contrast is so calculated that we are struck by the beauty of the composition of these settings.

In two scenes depicting Wakasa's relationship with Genjūrō, Mizoguchi's concern with the individual characters' movements becomes superbly effective, enhanced by the combined use of acoustics, makeup, and the high-angled camera. The first involves her seduction of Genjūrō. Her face is again made up like an immobile female Noh mask. The elderly attendant, attired in a black kimono, sits closest, showing her back to the camera. Her stature is as imposing as that of the princess herself, clad in a white kimono, seated as if to block Genjūrō, who is farthest from the camera. Sinister chimes—perhaps of a bell for Buddhist prayers—are heard intermittently. As Wakasa takes a drink of sake from a small wine cup, we hear the chime. When Genjūrō follows suit, we hear it again, as if to convince us that the bell marks each stage of his moral quandary. During the subsequent giving in—a loveplay chase—Mizoguchi makes sure that Wakasa stands high above Genjūrō whose lower position enhances a sense of his entrapment in her snares. The final shot shows him collapsing to the floor with her.

Needless to say, the soundtrack meantime becomes more dominant in order to reinforce the supernatural aura of this vignette. Wakasa's wedding song gradually merges with what sounds like a priest's low-toned prayer from a Noh play, accompanied by a wooden drum used for prayers. The camera quickly dollies from the center of the room to the corner to show us a suit of black armor, the source of the mysterious incantation. The voice is the spirit of Wakasa's father still haunting the mansion. The merging of songs of Wakasa and the spirit conjure up an image of death for the lovers' doomed affair.

Of course, this first scene of the lovers' union is more profitably viewed in relation to the second scene depicting Wakasa's anger at Genjūrō's desertion after he finds out that she is a ghost. Again, the camera's high angle and Wakasa's domineering posture heighten a sense of the still persistent snare from which Genjūrō is desperate to escape. Some discordant music combines with the princess Wakasa's black attire to further enhance the sinister atmosphere. The culmination of his struggle is shown in close-up from a high angle with the princess and her attendant looking reproachingly down at a sutra painted on Genjūrō's back. Here, we witness an interesting method for revealing Wakasa's true identity to him: shot-by-shot alternations.[11]

Two other important sequences reveal the outstanding quality of Mizoguchi's stylistic means for expressing Genjūrō's moral conflict. One is the sequence of the lovers' bathing and their subsequent repose on the lawn. This represents the culmination of Genjūrō's passion. Here Mizoguchi's cinematic rubric of the mood is superbly enhanced by the exquisite camera movement and pictorial filmic composition. Genjūrō is soaking himself in the spring while Wakasa is still ashore. Holding her hands, he tells her that he has never had such a wonderful experience. The camera follows Wakasa as she momentarily steps into the woods to take off her clothes and comes back to him. At the moment when they are about to embrace in the spring, Mizoguchi's camera moves uneasily, as Joan Mellen points out.[12] It quickly moves away from them and ends with a dissolve, as if to say that the director himself is averting his eyes from this spectacle of moral disarray. This traveling pan is in strong contrast with the earlier slow following shots, which imply Mizoguchi's sympathy for both Ohama and Miyagi. It is also counterpoised with a diagonal following shot which Mizoguchi uses to register approval of Genjūrō's repentance over his moral degradation, when he finds himself in the ruins of the mansion and thinks of starting homeward back to Miyagi.

After the dissolve that ends the scene at the spring, the camera dollies toward the bushes of a garden with raked white sand, and then moves up to show a long shot of Genjūrō and Wakasa on the lawn. The garden looks like the stone garden of Ryōanji or that of Daisenin Temple. An extremely brief shot of the garden whose effect is that of a kind of shock, is charged with a philosophical undertone: the garden stands by itself, transcending all petty human affairs.

Next Wakasa and Genjūrō are seen having a picnic on a blanket spread on the lawn, flooded with warm spring sunlight. The shot itself is pictorially beautiful, and the very essence of Mizoguchi's lyricism. The abrupt transition from the shadow in the bath scene to the light with the short stasis in between, and from closed framing to open framing as well, creates a kind of leisurely visual pleasure. This long shot persists. Genjūrō begins chasing Wakasa. The couple, clad in very light silk kimonos, look like two fluttering butterflies merging with the spring air. This take is one of the most memorable examples of Mizoguchi's skill at creating atmosphere. The romantic mood soon becomes tinged with an ominous undertone, however, when Genjūrō catches Wakasa and kisses her. The sound of bells returns, marking for us another stage in his moral crisis. Then a combination of discordant harp music and intermittent bells registers Genjūrō's indulgence in unbridled passion.

The other stylistically exquisite sequence comes toward the end of the film. Here Mizoguchi once more resorts to mood to present the typical quality of the Mizoguchi woman: the nobly forgiving source of the most rewarding form of redemption known to man. As in many other scenes, the transition from natural to supernatural is made so surreptitiously that the audience is again thrown into a state of shock, as Audie Bock points out.[13] When Genjūrō comes home, he enters the dark, deserted house. He goes out through the back door, and when the camera cuts to the interior next, we are surprised to see Miyagi (whom we saw killed) sitting near the brightly burning hearth. After the husband and child are asleep, the slowly moving camera and extreme low-key photography yield a mixture of tenderness and eeriness: the typical Mizoguchi mood.

Only a tiny spot of light from Miyagi's candle moves from place to place as she moves around the house, while the rest of the screen is dominated by darkness. We see her starting to patch her husband's kimono—the gesture indicative of female caring, her smiling face meeting the darkness.

We are now prepared for the final scene of the film, which brings its issues to resolution. Our vision of the world view in *Ugetsu* is enhanced by the liquid camera movement whose effect is again that of unfolding a picture scroll. The camera moves here from the particular to the general, in contrast to its movement in the opening sequence.

The exterior of the potter's house, formerly barren, is first presented. It has now changed into a farm which Tōbei is tilling. The camera follows the little boy going toward his mother's tomb and stops as he kneels before it. It then pans up and travels across the field to show the entire community. Thus its movement offers us a moment for reflection on the effect of war upon the lives of the four persons and their entire village. Here we come to accept that in time of civil war two conflicting ways of adapting to the environment were equally impossible to realize. The film's world view is basically ironic: no matter how an individual internalizes his motives, he cannot win. His survival is simply dependent upon chance. Miyagi's option, with which Mizoguchi sympathizes most, turns out to be less rewarding than the options taken by the others. Although Tōbei, Genjūrō, and Ohama have been defeated in their aims, they have survived; their very defeat has taught them the futility of all "options." This knowledge itself is their only reward; they will have to channel it into some significant action in the future.

A traveling shot of the entire village seems to imply a deeper philosophical idea, the concept of *mujō* (the mutability of all earthly phenomena), which must emerge from the film's final analysis. There are two important elements that make this vision possible. One is Princess Wakasa's singing, introduced twice in the film. At the wedding Wakasa sings: "The best of silk of choicest hue / May change and fade away, / As could my life, beloved one, / if thou shouldst prove untrue." The same song is recalled by Genjūrō, as he roams around the ramparts of the mansion. Her song certainly points to the transitoriness of all human affairs, a theme which underlies most of traditional Japanese art and literature.

The other important element is the rotating wheel, which is also presented twice, aided by the director's subtle evocation of mood. In the earlier scene, which is permeated by the cozy domestic atmosphere, both Genjūrō and Miyagi spin the potter's wheel in time with some light music. In the later scene, which depicts the serenely peaceful atmosphere after the civil war, Genjūrō spins the wheel alone, while his deceased wife's voice is heard encouraging him to make good pottery. Time, symbolized by the wheel, transcends all these human affairs. In a large span of time they comprise only one insignificant spot.

In the final shot we see the hitherto uninhabited landscape of the field with a few farmers tilling the soil. The complete harmony of the characters with their surroundings thus evokes a sense of regeneration. The tensions of war and ease of peace in the future are thus presented as part of a cyclical pattern working itself out in the fullness of time.

祇園囃子

9

Two Prolific Years: from *Gion Festival Music* to *The Crucified Lovers* (1953-54)

Confidence Regained

AFTER *UGETSU*, Mizoguchi's next four films show a steady, consistent mastery in marked contrast to the ups and downs of his previous career. *Gion Bayashi* (*Gion Festival Music* or *A Geisha*, 1953) was set in the Gion pleasure district. Working on a theme with which he felt comfortable, Mizoguchi was in complete control of the subject matter. The film was a good, mature work.

Mizoguchi followed it with a screen adaptation of "Sanshō Dayū" ("Sanshō the Bailiff"), a short story by Ōgai Mori. The world of historical legend as depicted by a leading intellectual novelist of the Meiji era would seem to be basically incompatible with the female-oriented world of Mizoguchi, yet he wanted to challenge that world view. From first to last, Mizoguchi set himself the task of looking past the romanticized image of women directly into the heart of the matter: the sacrifice of women to the dreams and convenience of a man's world. *Sanshō Dayū*, (*Sanshō the Bailiff*, 1954) won him the San Marco Silver Lion award at the 1954 Venice Film Festival.

Mizoguchi then moved on to *Uwasa no Onna* (*The Woman of the Rumor*, 1954). Set in the Shimabara licensed quarters, a familiar locale, this film portrayed the conflict between traditional and modern attitudes toward women and pleasure. Though not a first-rate work, *The Woman of the Rumor* shows once again how steady a hand Mizoguchi could bring to his art, given a congenial subject matter set in a familiar environment.

His next film, *Chikamatsu Monogatari* (*The Crucified Lovers*, 1954), is a masterly work shot in just thirty days. The material here was traditional: a seventeenth-century Bunraku play, *Daikyōji Mukashi-goyomi* (*The Almanac-Maker's Tale*) by Monzaemon Chikamatsu. Mizoguchi, as we shall see, knew just what he wanted, and how to go about doing it.

happy moment in Gion Festival Music *(1953): Miyoharu*
chiyo Kogure, left) and Eiko (Ayako Wakao).

Gion Bayashi (*Gion Festival Music*, 1953)

The soft, sure touch of Mizoguchi's late period is especially noticeable in *Gion Festival Music*, a virtual remake of the 1936 *Sisters of the Gion*. The emotional intensity of Omocha's curse on the profession of the geisha at the end of the earlier film has given way to a more accepting view. The stylistic rigor, especially the camera's dispassionate long look on the two sisters, has mellowed. Mizoguchi does not overwork his style; there are many close-ups and varieties of shot lengths. Nor is there the incessant returning to the dark, sunless alley by way of directing our thoughtful gaze at the felt reality of the sisters' life. What replaces these qualities is Mizoguchi's experienced portrayal of geisha and customers in the traditional pleasure quarters. The effect is that of a film of manners. Mizoguchi has relaxed.[1] A spirit of confrontation has yielded to one of less critical observation.

Even so, in both films Mizoguchi deals with the theme he has labored on for so long: the sacrifice of women in a money-dominated, male-oriented society. Again, the characters act out the woman's choice (or nonchoice) between conformity and rebellion. Conformity in this film is studied through a geisha's obligation to her proprietress, a kind of surrogate mother with absolute power to make or break the women she employs.

In *Sisters of the Gion,* Mizoguchi's commitment to polarity was much stronger. Omocha and Umekichi each stood for the contrary, and extreme, mode of choosing in a situation intolerable anyway. However, the two geisha in *Gion Festival Music* are shown to be more flexible in their sense of values and methods of survival. Miyoharu, the elder, is the traditional type who tries to be faithful to the accepted norms of geisha society. She fulfills her sense of *giri* ("social obligation") by taking in Eiko, daughter of her ex-patron, now destitute, and a fellow geisha, now dead. Eiko is a more modern type, a geisha who chooses her profession of her own free will, for reasons of economic independence. The two women's values first contrast, then merge, and are brought into open conflict and finally reconciled. A kind of wisdom of awareness of the limitation of self-assertiveness leads them to reconcile themselves to their lives.

The narrative focus on this progress toward wisdom and reconciliation is matched by some familiar expressive devices used to acquaint us with the peculiar atmosphere and customs of the geisha's life.

The film begins with such a device. A set of high-angled, reverse-field shots, along with a lateral dolly, discloses a little alley in the Gion district. Eiko walks with a bundle toward and away from the camera, then across the screen, looking for Miyoharu's house. As in *Sisters of the*

Gion, Mizoguchi uses this alley view as a leitmotiv throughout. In the earlier film, this image, with its associations of sunless damp, invited a thoughtful comparison with the felt life of the poverty-stricken geisha sisters. Here, the rhetorical undertone is different. The alley suggests snugness, coziness, and quietude of a sort which we can imagine is characteristic of the Gion in its "off hours." Then, too, houses like Miyoharu's are small but decent, and are cared for by servants. A woman vendor from Ohara, dressed in quaint local costume (a tourist attraction in Kyoto), walks through the alley. Her figure is wonderfully effective in creating the leisurely atmosphere of a summer afternoon when everything is at rest before the busy nightlife begins. Mizoguchi's rather slow camera movement, which corresponds to Eiko's as she examines the door plates one after another, also adds to this feeling.

Similarly, while an alley scene was used earlier as a prelude to dramatic events unfolding in the sisters' house, it now functions on two thematic levels; it prepares us for moral conflict and, as well, becomes the scene of dramatically important events. For example, after the proprietress of a prestigious geisha house has dismissed Miyoharu and Eiko, a group of young geisha gather round Eiko to console her. Setting this scene in the alley enlarges our sense of the geisha's life by domesticating the pleasure district more completely than before.

The opening sequence of *Gion Festival Music* offers the donnée for the two women's moral growth: Miyoharu's decision to serve as a guarantor for Eiko and train her to become a *maiko* ("young geisha"). The first half of the film develops contrasts between the two types of women adapting to their surroundings.

Miyoharu's protective nature is put in the foreground; she borrows money to buy kimonos for Eiko's debut as a *maiko*; and she chaperones her protégé to various geisha houses. Still unaccustomed to the ways of the world, Eiko displays her modern spirit. She refuses to see her father—the typical Mizoguchi improvident male who has delegated parental authority to someone else, in this case Miyoharu. Eiko flatly tells the proprietress Okimi that she will not have a patron unless she loves him.

Mizoguchi seems especially anxious to give us an inside view of life in the Gion. Details urge themselves on us with the special persuasiveness of effects arranged by an old habitué. At Miyoharu's house, the male servant and the maid are constantly seen in the background, answering the phone and helping the two geisha get dressed. At one point, it is the male servant who tightens Miyoharu's sash. Sometimes these everyday details add telling reinforcement to the theme of oppressive role-playing, as when Miyoharu meets the proprietress Okimi who has such power over her life and Eiko's, and asks for a loan. Miyoharu sits upright in the posture becoming a geisha and a lady, while Okimi lounges at ease wearing white *tabi* socks suitable for a kimono, and a Western summer dress—an odd combination which passes for casual wear in the Gion. In a similar vein, we follow Miyoharu into her kitchen where the modest fixtures and old charcoal brazier reveal a perhaps unexpected degree of frugality in the household of a fashionable geisha.

The action of the film changes radically in the second half. Again it is money which forces Miyoharu to yield to an unpleasant fulfillment of *giri* ("obligation"). Using a loan from the wealthy customer Kusuda for leverage, Okimi forces Miyoharu and Eiko to accompany Kusuda's party to Tokyo. Yet this compromise unites the two women in a determined resistance to exploitation. Eiko refuses the advances of Kusuda, who wants to be her patron and bites his lips so badly that he has to be hospitalized. Miyoharu is unwilling to sleep with Kanzaki, the government official whom Kusuda is trying to bribe. However, their only challenge to the values of the Gion district manipulated by money and men is costly. Okimi, enraged, stops using their services.

Cut off from their sole source of income, Miyoharu and Eiko must shift ground. Again, the motif of protection is presented at a quick pace with varied shots. The maid, answering the phone, informs Miyoharu that Eiko is now with Okimi, apologizing for her conduct. A close-up shows Miyoharu on the phone pleading with Okimi not to send Eiko to Kusuda. A long shot of Miyoharu going to the mirror and fixing her face quickly indicates the urgency of the situation. The festival music sounds in the distance, ironically, as if to signal Miyoharu's return to compromise: she will make herself available to the corrupt government officials to save Eiko.

Before Miyoharu's and Eiko's final reconciliation with their fate, Mizoguchi brings their confrontation to a full climax. He lets us see it from various angles, sometimes emphasizing their psychological plight and at others stressing the circumstances of their conflict. As might be expected, shot size and angle vary accordingly. The alley which Miyoharu enters, carrying several packages, prepares us for the dramatic highpoint. Inside the house, Eiko rejects the packages, gifts for her, which Miyoharu apparently has bought with the money she received for her services to Kanzaki. A series of close-ups of Eiko finally explores her awareness of the dark side of the geisha's profession: "If you have to sell yourself for survival, I'll quit. Sister, you should get out of this profession."

Miyoharu's pent-up indignation at the contradictions inherent in her environment also prompts her to take some decisive action: she slaps the younger woman's face. The camera follows Eiko to a corner of the room and cuts to a close-up. From this point on, Miyoharu's feelings are expressed by her gestures as well as her talk from the camera's considerable distance. A high-angle long shot of her folding a sash conveys a sense of her resignation to the oppressive environment of which she is part and parcel. A ninety-degree pan shows Miyoharu approaching Eiko. Next, a rather long take of the two together draws our attention to the nobility of the elder's self-sacrifice. For the first time, Miyoharu expresses her affection for the younger at length: she wants to save Eiko's chastity at her own cost; she has disposed of all her valuable jewelry to help Eiko's father. Saying that she considers Eiko a real sister since she has no close kin, she walks screen right, leaving the girl alone.

Next, a cut from Miyoharu in the other room takes us to the maid in the kitchen, who has been listening in on the domestic discord all this while, fanning herself.[2] Rather than offering dramatic relief, this take reveals another dimension of life in the Gion. The old maid, who has been serving Miyoharu for a long time, has seen and accepted the joys and sorrows of the geisha's life in a matter-of-fact way. There is no inquisitiveness or dismay in her attitude.

Eiko suddenly crosses in front of the maid and rushes to Miyoharu. The camera moves with her all the way and stops to celebrate the mutual understanding in their embrace. From this point on, the film quickly picks up pace. The old maid is busily answering phone calls from various tea houses requesting the two women's services. Miyoharu fixes Eiko's makeup, and they cheerfully step out of the house. The image of the alley again suggests a sense of cozy snugness and provides a moment for reflection. We think how a spirit of compromise has brought them to a new understanding of one another and of their lives. As they walk down the street together, the Gion Festival music and floats seem to celebrate their new consciousness of being ready to face their world on its own terms.

Yet undercutting a sense of settlement reaffirmed by the alley image and promise of hope echoed by the joyous festival music, the film's ending also suggests a message stated more explicitly in *Sisters of the Gion*: the existence of a larger impersonal world outside, where female sacrifice like the geisha's is taken for granted. Omocha cursed it and Umekichi, in tears, endured it; now Miyoharu and Eiko accept it, ready to make the best of a bad bargain, by affirming a mother-daughter/elder sister–younger sister bond as the source of their strength.

Sanshō Dayū (Sanshō the Bailiff, 1954)

Sanshō the Bailiff is a social vision of twelfth-century Japan, that "dark age when people did not fully know what it meant to be human."[3] Like *Ugetsu*, the film investigates the individual's coming to terms with an oppressive feudal structure. By introducing the motif of the protagonist Zushiō's roaming, Mizoguchi manages to deal with the conflicting value orientations of people from different social backgrounds.

Zushiō's father, a local governor, represents moral integrity. His attempts to secure farmers their rights runs counter to the wishes of the central regime and causes his exile. The film deals with the consequences for his family of this good man's downfall. The film takes its title from the villain in the piece. Sanshō the bailiff is the direct opposite of the governor; he is corrupt and the model for the exploitative official.

Zushiō's younger sister, Anju, like their father, is associated with high moral standards. However, the depressing conditions of slavery into which she is thrust have diminished her will to effect positive changes in the world. Just as her father sacrificed his political career, and eventually his life, for a principle, Anju gives her life in an act of self-sacrifice for Zushiō.

Zushiō's mother, Tamaki, on the other hand, exemplifies the will to survive so conspicuously lacking in her husband and daughter. When she tries to escape from the brothel to which she has been sold, she finds out how impossible it is to change her fate by fighting in an unsupportive environment. Even so, her subsequent resignation to fate, though fraught with torment and defeat, is relieved by a streak of hope—the hope of being united with her children.

The slaves whom Mizoguchi treats as a collective entity have a similar orientation to an extremely hostile environment. However, while Tamaki's resignation can be directed toward the future, that of the slaves is completely hopeless. They have been part of the oppressive feudal structure for so long that when freedom does arrive, they are at a loss to know what to do with it.

Tarō, Sanshō's oldest son, offers another dimension of this scheme of values: escapism. Ashamed of his father's cruel enslavement of human beings, he rebels against the paternal authority by entering the priesthood. However, this option is not available to unfortunates like Anju, for whom death is the only escape.

Mizoguchi studies these complexities of human choice in relation to the maturing process of the young hero, Zushiō. This central theme moves from separation to reunion as he shifts ground in value systems over a period of ten years. Significantly, Mizoguchi lays stress on the naturalistic forces molding the individual's character throughout. The father has taught the son this maxim: "A man without pity is no longer human." However, conditions in a slave camp force Zushiō to recognize the value of expediency or opportunism. He dares to brand a runaway slave, an old man, who wanted only a taste of freedom before his death. Here, Mizoguchi's familiar device returns: a noble woman comes to the rescue with an act of supreme self-sacrifice. Zushiō is the man helped to his goal by a sister so devoted that she gives her life so that he can escape the slave labor camp.

The film takes a new turn as Zushiō finds himself free to grow in moral stature. With good fortune and pluck he prospers, rising to the rank of governor over the province where Sanshō's vast slave camp is situated. Given high office, Zushiō finds reason in his past shifting values to dedicate himself to bettering the lot of the oppressed. Following his father's example, he issues a decree freeing all the slaves in the province. Yet he is caught on the horns of a dilemma. His decree is both right and wrong: morally right in the sense of serving the public good; and wrong in the sense that it proves incompatible with the rule of the central government, and therefore contributes to instability. This conflict of dedication to the public good causes Zushiō to resign from his post.

Having failed to improve the social order, he turns to a more privately meaningful righting of wrongs: he sets out in search of his mother. The mutual caring of mother and son turns out to be the reward of Zushiō's quest. This basic given of human solidarity, though a commonplace as in many of Kurosawa's films, is presented as the only possible point of reference for human values powerful enough to mitigate the pain of living in such a benighted world.

As so often before, Mizoguchi enriches his theme with some powerfully evocative touches all his own. Clearly, his sympathies lie with the nobly fallen women driven by forces beyond their control and for the enslaved masses. Mizoguchi knows exactly how to let his (or Miyagawa's) camera do the talking in order to give the spectacle of human pathos its appropriate artistic/emotive contour.

Such is the scene depicting the journey of Tamaki and her children Zushiō and Anju soon after the father's exile. Accompanied by their old maid, they are on their way to the then remote island of Kyūshū to join him. A high-angled camera is fixed on the four as they thread their way through tall pampas grass waving in the sunlight. The pictorially exquisite composition creates a mixture of responses. Their light, almost floating steps in rhythm with the waving grass suggest an identification with the world of nature. This harmony, along with the prevailing white tones and their joyous talk, is in keeping with the happy mood appropriate to the expected reunion with the father. However, the camera's high angle and the open framing (which suggests the vast stretch of the marsh) subtly undercut this mood, conveying a sense of oppression and forlornness shared by the women and the children amid the hardship of the traveling.

This lyrical texture yields to the stark severity of the slave camp. Low-key photography and the high-angle long shot prevail here. The

Sanshō the Baliff: Tamaki (Kinuyo Tanaka) is to be hamstrung
for attempting to escape from a brothel.

slaves are shown surrounded by tall latticelike stockades. They are
entirely absorbed by the dismal sunless settings, which reduce them to
fixtures of an environment. Even without resorting to a close-up,
Mizoguchi submerges us in this atmosphere; we experience something
of the torpid misery of masses of human beings caged like animals.

Mizoguchi also alternates shots depicting the horrors of slavery. For
example, the branding of an old runaway is presented in a medium shot.
Significantly, as was shown in the famous bathing scene in *Ugetsu*,
Mizoguchi's camera moves firmly away when Zushio takes up the red hot
iron, as if to express the director's own disgust with the young man's
breach of humane behavior. In the scene where the guards of the brothel
make ready to cut Tamaki's tendon after her escape attempt, the same
averting eye of the camera is used.

The lyrical poetic atmosphere again surfaces in the emotionally taut
scenes revealing women's suffering. The moment of Anju's heroic sacrifice is one such moment. To ensure Zushiō's escape, she misleads the
guards, running in the opposite direction. Her own flight is presented in
two long takes: a long shot of her running through the woods away from
the camera; and a medium shot of her advancing to the center of the
screen with the camera fixed on her.

Our sustained tension dissolves into an artistic shock as Anju's figure gradually fades out to be replaced by a shot of ripples spreading on the surface of a pond. Reminiscent of the image of the lake which engulfs the heroine and all her purity and impurity in the final scene of *A Picture of Madame Yuki*, this stasis enables us to see and feel Anju's plight in a more enriching way. All those inhuman aspects of the slave camps, associated with the clamorous wooden clappers and images of fire, are finally integrated in this final solemn image of heroic self-sacrifice.

Indeed, this merging of the mobile and immobile is a superb comment on Anju's fleeting life. While the ripples signify the dying moments of her life, the calming surface of the water powerfully connotes the impersonal law of *mujō*, the ephemerality of human affairs, always at work in the individual life.

An equally artistically controlled yet emotionally magnetizing scene is found after the episode involving the guards' cutting Tamaki's tendon. Aided by her fellow prostitutes, Tamaki reaches a remote promontory. As her sorrowful voice calls out for Anju and Zushiō in tune with the emotive tones of a *samisen,* the wind carries her voice away, as if her cries were destined to be scattered by the impersonal force of nature. The site is deserted save for a few pine trees, the main signs of life on this remote Sado Island (a place of exile in ancient times). Tamaki's single figure blends with the bleak surroundings, and this fusion, with its magnificently pictorial rendering, creates a mood appropriate for the pathos of motherly affection holding steadfast against all change of time and circumstance.

The camera follows attentively as she limps toward the ocean. Again, Mizoguchi is sensitive to body language; Tamaki's back, more effectively than her face, expresses the poor mother's nobility in enduring her fate. Her suffering climaxes when rising wind, the theme music, her cry, and the *samisen* tune (reminiscent of her heart's cry) all merge as if to echo through some vacuum extending out over the vast ocean.

Mizoguchi pours all his creative energy into the climactic final scene which brings the film's thematic conflict to resolution. The camera's alternating distance balances our identification and detachment. A long shot shows Zushiō walking along the deserted beach of Sado Island toward a half-demolished shack. Next, there is a shot of Tamaki, now an old woman crouching nearby, turning away from the camera. We see immediately that the thin line of shoulder conspicuous through her tattered kimono is an index of her felt life. The camera, from a reverse-field angle, reveals more aspects of her declining fortunes; she is now blind and is chasing away birds with a stick, while still calling out for her children. Her wailing voice is a heroic display of the love of which this old woman is still capable, undefeated by her circumstances. Zushiō clings to Tamaki, calling her mother. However, the next close-up of her face ironically discloses a bitterness that has developed thanks to a dehumanizing environment. She tells him not to tease an old woman and leaves him alone (in frame).

Another appropriate rescue device comes in here: a small image of the goddess of mercy left with Zushiō by his father. Toward the end, the camera gradually tracks up to Zushiō approaching his mother. A medium shot of Tamaki touching the statue is taken over by a close-up celebrating mother-son reunion in their embrace. The lyrical music of a Japanese flute joins this celebration. The camera tracks away a little, and keeps its long, high-angled look on them while they recount their past experiences.

Our happy/sad immersion in mother and son is suddenly lifted to a plane of contemplative detachment as the camera, still with the same angle, moves away to the left to show an old sea-weed gatherer engaged in his task. The film ends with a stasis: the beach with heaps of sea-weed swept up by the waves. The various water images—the pond which engulfed Anju, the deserted ocean over which the mother's cry for her children died away—are finally consummated in this image from the sea. Here there is a rhythm of life, a sense of the restoration of the natural order, as signified by the sea-weed. Obviously, the metaphor is pertinent for the beginning of a new life for mother and son built on the wreckage of their experience. The final stasis convincingly suggests the existence of the universal law, *mujō* (the callous progression of time) which ultimately transcends the human sense of loss and thus of hope and despair. Yet we are left troubled with sad thoughts about the future of Zushiō and Tamaki because our sense of tragic loss remains, willy-nilly, so acute.

Uwasa no Onna (*The Woman of the Rumor*, 1954)

In *The Woman of the Rumor*, the dramatic tautness which sparkled in *Sanshō the Bailiff* has given way to a kind of relaxed quality something like slackness. The film draws on earlier works such as *Gion Festival Music* and *Sisters of the Gion* in theme and character. Set in the Shimabara District, a traditional licensed red-lantern district of Kyoto, the film concerns the relationship between two women, this time mother and daughter. Confrontation with the environment here means coping with the business of managing a brothel. As in the case of *Gion Festival Music*, the contrasting value systems are set in opposition with some degree of flexibility. The widowed mother, Hatsuko, is the owner of a first-rate brothel called Izutsuya. She considers her profession as a means of survival for her and her girls as well; she is in fact proud of the financial success which has given her daughter a college education and herself purchase on a kind of "respectability." The daughter, Yukiko, a "modern" type, is ashamed of her mother's profession since it involves human exploitation and reflects on her respectability.

Like Miyoharu and Eiko in *Gion Festival Music*, Hatsuko and Yukiko are shown first in contrast, then brought into open conflict and ultimately reconciled. Undoubtedly, it is the medical doctor, Matoba, Hatsuko's lover, who instigates the mother-daughter conflict.

Thus *The Woman of the Rumor* concerns the two women's coming to grips with the limits which society puts on their power to set themselves goals and achieve them. Mizoguchi returns to his expressive methods, highly accentuated this time by Western cinematic devices: close-ups, intercutting, and many reverse-field shots. Though there are a few instances of dollying and long takes, these are relegated to the background.

The film opens with a high angle shot of the street in front of the Izutsuya brothel. A spacious entryway impresses us immediately with a sense of affluence. As before in *Gion Festival Music*, Mizoguchi brings us here in the leisure off-hours of the district. He even uses the same touch of local color as before, introducing a female vendor from Ohara into the leisurely traffic of pedestrians. Yet this smugly prosperous atmosphere is subtly undercut by a high angle view of a traditional architectural feature of the Japanese brothel: the oppressively serried stretch of lattice windows along the second floor. This touch of claustrophobia is strengthened by the arrival of a taxi. Yukiko gets out, wearing a black dress and looking exceedingly melancholy. She hurries in. She has failed in a suicide attempt in Tokyo after her fiancé discovered her mother's profession.

The film proceeds to offer a study in contrasts as the privileged daughter of the house is shown in relation to the girls who earn their living there. Yukiko is presented in a chic Western dress while the courtesans wear gaudy traditional finery and thick makeup. The girls gather together to eat a traditional yet skimpy breakfast, while Yukiko's meal consists of specially prepared egg and toast. Her spacious room has a piano, a sewing machine, and comfortable Western furniture while the girls crowd together in a low-ceilinged room upstairs.

Mizoguchi uses an interesting deep focus and decentering device for contrasting Hatsuko's rooms with the living quarters of her girls. The madame's gracious three rooms with attractive partitions and fresh floor mats are made to seem even more splendid by an elegant dressing mirror occupying the lower part of the screen. People moving in and out cross the upper screen, moving into the lower for dramatic interaction.

We cannot help but notice the spacious neatness of these quarters, especially since a similar division of the screen is used to show us the shabby single room occupied by Hatsuko's girls. Here, people pass in and out in the upper portion of the screen, entering the lower half to interact in the cramped confines of a sickbed quilt laid out to accommodate the ailing courtesan, Usuyuki Dayū. The contrast is telling, a matter of narrow quarters and depressing wear and tear. The worn floor mats, low ceiling, small lattice windows, and workaday female clutter say enough about working conditions in a house where girls toil so the proprietress may flourish.

Hatsuko's means of buying "true respectability" is through the physician Matoba, her secret, and much younger, lover. By mortgaging her brothel to help him open his clinic, Hatsuko is willing to risk her financial independence for a prospect of marriage. In order to dramatize her sense of insecurity, Mizoguchi brings in a touch of grim humor—something rarely seen in his other films. At the theater where she and Matoba are watching a group of young geisha dancing, the fickle Matoba is searching his program, anxious to identify two girls to his liking. A medium shot of Hatsuko closing the program and pinching him cuts to a close-up of the geisha on the stage. The contrast between youth and old age—one factor Hatsuko cannot ignore—is pointed.

In another scene at the Noh theater, Hatsuko eavesdrops on a conversation between Matoba and Yukiko who have become intimate. In the lobby they are planning to go up to Tokyo together, since Yukiko is unaware of her mother's involvement with Matoba. Betrayed and angered, Hatsuko returns to her seat inside and watches a *kyōgen* ("comic interlude"). Ironically, the piece is about an old woman infatuated with a young man. The camera cuts back and forth, often in close-up, between the actors on the stage and Hatsuko suppressing indignation, Matoba looking serious, or Yukiko laughing. The comically infatuated old hag now enters the stage, carrying a pillow, her gaudy underwear sticking out of her kimono. Amid the audience's gales of laughter, the camera cuts to a close-up of Hatsuko to finalize her humiliation. She leaves in a hurry.

This episode brings us to the culmination of the triangular relationship in which the daughter first learns about Matoba's involvement with her mother. In a fashion typical of the *shinpa* melodrama, Mizoguchi lets Matoba's and Hatsuko's posture express their subtly changing feelings. The camera's long look rests on them as Hatsuko's initial threats lapse into a humble plea to win Matoba back. Both of them stand; Hatsuko sits down and Matoba follows suit; she clings to him, as he becomes firmer, persuading her to calm down; finally they stand up. The daughter steps out of the room. The scene ends with a shot of Hatsuko's empty room, an

In The Woman of the Rumor, *the middle-aged Hatsuko (Kinuyo
Tanaka) becomes involved with a cunning young physician
(Tomoemon Ōtani).*

obvious invitation to consider the future of these three people as hanging in the balance.

Hatsuko courageously offers to sacrifice herself for the happiness of her daughter and Matoba. She gives him the check intended for his clinic and asks him to take good care of Yukiko. Even so, the mother's great-hearted sacrifice does not end the matter happily.

Mizoguchi prolongs the moral conflict of the three in a different setting and through different techniques. When the camera cuts to Yukiko's room, Matoba is asking her to go to Tokyo with him. She replies that it is cruel of him to think of building success and happiness on his exploitation of her mother. This time, a set of reverse-field shots contrasts and compares the accuser and the accused facing one another. Their confrontation ends when Yukiko grabs a pair of scissors to attack Matoba. She is stopped by her mother who hurries in. Matoba leaves.

Both mother and daughter are losers now. But this sense of defeat is itself a kind of reward. It teaches them something about the inadequacy of their commitment and something about male egotism. It also strengthens the mother-daughter bond. Yet Yukiko is still anxious to begin a new life as a piano teacher in Tokyo. However, a daughter's independence must be subordinated to her sense of obligation to her mother. This is brought about by a convenient melodramatic ploy: Hatsuko's sudden illness. The film is weakened by the resulting sudden and gratuitous shift in Yukiko's motivation. Again reverse-field setup returns to show Yukiko busily managing the brothel in her ailing mother's place. Yukiko's acceptance of the mother's values is evidenced by a customer's comment that she is the temporary new madame.

Mizoguchi does approach a statement on the subject of prostitution, though only in the final sequence. A courtesan, thickly madeup, is ready to go out to entertain her customers. Unlike Omocha who cursed her profession in *Sisters of the Gion,* this girl sighs and asks: "Can our profession ever disappear?"

Clearly, Mizoguchi builds his answer on a circular pattern. Chiyo, a younger sister of the deceased Usuyuki Dayū, was once discouraged by Yukiko from becoming a courtesan; now she returns to follow in her sister's footsteps. And of course we now see Yukiko (temporarily) replacing her mother. The film ends as it began, with a shot of the street in front of the Izutsuya brothel. This time, in place of a female vendor in a quaint kimono, we see a young woman in Western dress accosting customers. Obviously, Mizoguchi is saying that, despite the process of modernization, women's need to make their desirability pay must continue in one form or another. Here in the final coda, neither Mizoguchi's criticism of social inequity nor his sympathy for its female victims shows through. This is a Mizoguchi content to look at life with some degree of detachment—and to show us plainly how it is.

Chikamatsu Monogatari (*The Crucified Lovers,* 1954)

The Crucified Lovers, like *Utamaro and His Five Women,* is Mizoguchi's celebration of tragic love. Taking up the subject of adultery in the merchant class of seventeenth-century feudal Japan, he shows us how the variables of external circumstances can work together to drive an innocent man and woman to destruction.

The outstanding quality of this film is Mizoguchi's ability to give a lucid psychological density to two lovers trapped in their fate. Furthermore, Mizoguchi brings a unique modern interpretation, a transcendent world view, to the final resolution of the issues involved. His familiar stylistic devices—the one-scene, one-shot method, pictorial composition, and *bunraku* chanting—are all used to achieve a marvel of narrative concentration. Moreover, he brings something new to his technique of psychological enrichment by paying special attention to the vertical movement of characters shot with extreme economy and a certain studied avoidance of his famous dollying and panning.

The Crucified Lovers begins with an almost impatient assembling of the forces which bring the socially incompatible hero and heroine together only to destroy them. As evidenced by films such as *Ugetsu* and *Sisters of the Gion,* Mizoguchi is famous for the liquid flow of the camera in the opening sequence. However, *The Crucified Lovers* opens with a series of brief shots, aimed at breaking our sense of spatial and temporal continuity. A high angle shot of Ishun, an affluent scrollmaker, outside his house quickly cuts to the interior when he hurries in. He is up against a deadline for the annual calendar (source of his prosperity) whose publication he wants to monopolize. A number of shots exhibit the division of labor as performed by workers in different sections of the house. Another set of shots takes us to the attic where the foreman Mohei, the hero, is roused out of sickbed to touch up the calendar.

Ishun remarks that he has bribed various impoverished court officials to get his monopoly. Referring to his master's miserliness, a clerk says that it is no good lecturing the work force on the morality of loyalty to the business when the master pays starvation wages.

These abrupt opening shots, of course, correspond to the hustle and bustle connected with the approaching deadline for publication. Money does indeed come to the fore because it is scrollmaker Ishun's sole means of social advancement in the feudal hierarchy. At the same time, as one critic notes, this "fragmentation of setting separates the characters from one another."[4] Thus we see at the outset how the rigorously vertical structure within the merchant's household faithfully reflects the social strata of feudal Japan. Against this background defined by money and mores, Osan appears, the wife of Ishun, and soon the ill-fated lover of Mohei. There is something about her posture which indicates that she is unhappy.

The role of money as a deterministic force is summed up in two scenes depicting Osan's moral crisis when Dōki, her elder brother, and Okō, her aged mother, come one after the other to solicit a loan to pay the scapegrace Dōki's pressing debts. These scenes confirm our initial suspicion that Osan's melancholy aspect reflects her unhappiness as the bartered bride of feudal times.

Osan is torn between two types of *giri* ("filial obligation"): loyalty to husband; and devotion to family. Caught as she is between two such incompatible demands, she appeals to the only person who can conceivably help her—Mohei, her husband's trusty foreman. Thus Mohei is also forced to choose between *giri* ("social obligation") and *ninjō* ("personal feelings"): his devotion to the absolute master and his concern for the helpless wife. He chooses the latter.

Osan's appeal to Mohei, the initial step toward their undoing, is rendered with calculated formal patterns. A short, single take is used to contain a wealth of action. Having sat up overnight to complete the calendar, Mohei wakes up from a short nap, ready to return to his room. Suddenly, Noh music is introduced to merge with a woman's voice calling his name. Osan walks down the corridor toward the camera and faces Mohei occupying the lower left corner. She asks him to come with her and walks away from the camera down the corridor. The vertical lines of the corridor and pillars, along with the walls and room partitions boxing in the attic gloom, enhance a feeling of oppressive confinement. We register a sense of entrapment, too, as Osan, attired in a black kimono, walks like a Noh performer, leading Mohei deeper into the shadows. There, we feel, he will be ensnared in an inescapable commitment.

Osan and Mohei are soon entangled in a web of incriminating circumstances. First, Mohei is caught in the act of using his master's seal to procure the money Osan needs for her brother. By giving in to blackmail by Sukeemon, the cunning clerk who has caught him, he could escape. Instead, he confesses to Ishun. First Osan, then the maid Otama attempt to intercede for him, the latter claiming that he did it for her, in order to save her sick aunt. This well-intended lie enrages Ishun all the more, since his lecherous advances to Otama have been forestalled by her equally spurious claim that she is Mohei's intended bride. After publicly humiliating Mohei, Ishun has him thrown into a locked storeroom.

Another set of incriminating circumstances develops around Osan's attempt to force an accommodation from her husband by catching him in a compromising situation. She waits in Otama's room where Ishun is expected to come sneaking in to make his advances. Unhappily, Mohei arrives instead. He has come to thank Otama for her noble gesture. The wily clerk Sukeemon catches and exposes the innocent pair.

Mizoguchi gives dramatic intensity to the first of these moral crises—Mohei's public humiliation—by combining variable shots and sound effects borrowed from the kabuki theater. In contrast to some other scenes, each shot is fast-paced to augment a sense of mounting stress. The scene begins with a series of long shots of Ishun subjecting Mohei to a public reprimand. Ishun stands high on the platform of the corridor leading into the house while Mohei is below him in the court-yard. Naturally, their relative positions emphasize the clear distinction between master and servant—one with especially sinister overtones in a society like this, in which offence given social superiors is punished with special severity. Thus we see Osan standing elevated above Mohei as well before the shot returns to Ishun demanding to know who put him up to this attempted forgery. Mohei will not answer. All we hear is a *samisen* playing loudly in the background. Ishun prepares to kick Mohei. A medium shot of the two men is varied when Otama steps up to say that Mohei did it for her.

The camera moves to the right to show Osan in close-up. Her face displays pain and consternation. There is a quick cut back to Ishun, Mohei, and Otama; the camera has now panned ninety degrees so that the corridor is perpendicular to the camera. Ishun leaves, ordering his men to lock up Mohei.

As we have seen, Osan's attempt to strike a balance with her husband, like Mohei's gratitude to Otama, results in the "lovers" being exposed in a false light. This has immediately disastrous consequences which, though thwarted for the moment, will return ineluctably later on. The first consequence of discovery is Mohei's loss once and for all of his master's confidence; though he succeeds in escaping from the house, he must perforce become an exile. Osan is offered escape of another sort: Ishun hands her the knife for a ritual suicide. Disgusted by this flagrant application of the double standard and knowing that she is innocent, she too takes flight.

Again, the couple are brought together by a twist of fate: Mohei comes upon Osan wandering the dark streets. She tells him of her vow never to return to Ishun's house. Unable to change her resolve, Mohei again does the noble thing: he agrees to see her safely on her way.

The second half of the film depicts the classical pattern of the "lovers'" journey, with its moments of joy and peril, brief separation, and ultimate reunion in death. Here, the pattern includes an ironic false climax of attempted double suicide.

The climactic scene is reminiscent of the famous boat journey in *Ugetsu*. There, three masterly long shots of a boat moving slowly across a lake are used, along with the one-scene, one-shot method, to achieve a thematic effect. Here, the boat scene is intended to dramatize a shift in the psychological schema of the film from a theme of constraint to one of freedom. Osan and Mohei become real lovers in this, their false last hour, when they have resolved to die honorably now that Ishun's henchmen are closing in.

Mizoguchi has taken great care to register a wealth of subtle detail in this moment of emotional rapture. After all, more is involved than a shared death wish: having declared their love, Osan and Mohei decide to live. The director's task is to show how a world of obstacles is met and overcome through this difficult, socially unacceptable decision. He does this partly by fixing his camera steadily on the couple for as long as several minutes in one shot, so that their movements create a system of connotations. Though the framework remains open, the dense fog surrounding the boat contributes an opposing effect of enclosure. This, like the camera's steadily intent gaze, fixes our attention on the slightest visual alteration. We also cannot help but be drawn into this scene by its sheer beauty of texture and composition: dark water and grey fog harmonize with Osan's black kimono and Mohei's striped clothing.

At first, Mohei's position in the boat suggests the difference in rank that has such tragic consequences for these two. He stops rowing and kneels to bind Osan's ankles in preparation for her suicide. However, with death so close, he forgets who he is. He confesses his love; he even places his hands on her knees. Osan, suddenly waking to love, abandons her death wish; she asks Mohei to hold her tightly.

Next we see them standing together, a clear sign that differences of class no longer matter.[5] The music of drum and bamboo flute crescendos. Mohei sits down. So does Osan. When she throws herself on him, the boat suddenly turns ninety degrees.[6] This movement is like the actor's sudden halt, or *merihari* device, whereby he signals action leading to decisive outcome. Here, it signifies that Mohei and Osan are now man and woman, not servant and mistress; they will live and love, even as fugitives.

The boat scene takes us to another emotionally charged confirmation of the lovers' bond. Here, stylistically, Mizoguchi has something different at hand. The scene is set in a mountain area where the couple

The famous love scene between Osan (Kyōko Kagawa) and Mohei (Kazuo Hasegawa) in The Crucified Lovers, *a classic example of Mizoguchi's one-scene, one-shot method.*

journey on their way to hide in the house of Mohei's father. This location allows a full use of the fluid crane movement. Furthermore, various sound effects from artificial and natural sources—bamboo clappers, the sinister drum, running water, and a warbling bird—establish an admixture of despair and joy appropriate to the emotive atmosphere.

An old woman returns to a little hut where Osan is resting, and asks her where Mohei is. After deciding to save Osan's honor, Mohei has secretly left her to have himself arrested and charged as her abductor. A close-up of the surprised Osan quickly yields to an extreme long shot of her running after Mohei in the distance hurrying along the mountain path. The camera's high angle and Osan's tiny figure against the vast stretch of the landscape convey a sense of complete dejection. Next, a long take shows Osan coming down the mountain from the upper portion of the screen. She stumbles. Again, the camera gazes intently at the postures assumed by the lovers. As Osan confesses that Mohei is her only true love, he stoops to kiss her feet. Then he moves around her; they embrace and fall to the ground.

The lovers are apprehended. Thanks to Ishun's bribery of influential court officials, Osan is taken home unpunished and put in her mother's custody. Mohei, however, is imprisoned in his father's little storage hut pending official transport back to Kyoto. The father sets his son free. From this moment on, Mohei's character grows progressively more heroic. When he sneaks into the garden of the house of Osan's mother to take "his lover" back, he is no longer submissive. Osan's mother, Okō, asks Mohei to leave immediately while the lovers sit facing her. Though inferior in status, Mohei firmly rejects Okō's request and even says that he has come to claim her daughter as his own. There is no mistaking the significance of the way Mohei draws himself up erect as he says this; or the way Osan looks admiringly up at him.[7] This time, the scene ends with a close-up of their embrace.

This shot works effectively to transmit a sense of final, fatal togetherness chiefly because of Mizoguchi's timely introduction of a huge lattice door in the hallway of Okō's house. The alert audience will immediately recognize its similarity to the door of an ancient prison. Mizoguchi presents it not once but twice—before and after the lovers' embrace. Accompanied by loud wooden clappers signaling impending danger, Osan's brother sneaks through the door to report Mohei's presence to the police to save his sister from punishment. Later, accompanied by the same sound effect, a group of officials steps in through the door. Thus, the lattice ends a long series of images of constraint: the gigantic barrels behind which Osan and Mohei hide while police officials search for them; the small windowlike exit of an inn where they manage to elude a police patrol; and the tiny bamboo shelter (with no window) where the lovers spend their last night together before Mohei's arrest.

Mohei's and Osan's arrest and their confession of adultery lead to the final coda. Here, the action of the film shifts drastically again, as yet another kind of liberation is achieved. This section contains a crane shot of Osan and Mohei, tied together on horseback, being driven through the streets on their way to crucifixion. At the beginning of the film, together with Mohei and Osan, we have seen two adulterers from different classes—a samurai's wife and a servant—led to execution. However, this circular pattern lets us see Mohei's and Osan's predicament in a more illuminating way.

The medium shot following the crane shot shows them bound back to back. While the condemned in the earlier scene sat immobile, Mohei and Osan turn their heads to smile at each other. An onlooker, one of Osan's maids, says that she has never seen her mistress look so happy. Here, Mizoguchi uses a powerful low angle shot—rarely used in this film—as if to vent emotion in a kind of admiring celebration of the lovers' courage in accepting death in order to be reunited in heaven. The wooden clappers (from the kabuki stage) and traditional Japanese music add to this effect so that the tragedy of the crucified lovers ends on a note of joy, of genuine transcendence.

10

Last Years / Last Films (1955–56)

Physical Decline

THE LAST brief phase of Mizoguchi's career began with a characteristic irony: international success brought honors and recognition, along with the distractions of fame and the failing health which together helped spoil his last three films.

Mizoguchi's first venture was unhappy from the start. The script for *Yōkihi* (*The Princess Yang Kwei-fei*, 1955) dealt with the Chinese aristocracy of the eighth century. Mizoguchi ought to have known better than to put himself on such unfamiliar ground; he had failed that way so often before. However, this project was urged on him by the Daiei Company acting in concert with the Shaw Brothers of Hong Kong. The production proved vexing in the usual ways, with changes of script and scriptwriters (four in all), and sets and actresses as well.

The failure was followed by another period film in color, *Shin Heike Monogatari* (*New Tales of the Taira Clan*, 1955). Mizoguchi's reputation had brought him a seat on the board of directors of the Daiei Company, and he had received a Purple Ribbon Medal given by the government for his contribution to the Japanese film industry. By this time he knew that he was seriously ill, but not yet that he had leukemia. *New Tales of the Taira Clan*, in any case, was not a successful work. His scriptwriter Yoda claims that Mizoguchi showed little interest in it.

Akasen Chitai (*Street of Shame*, 1956) was to be Mizoguchi's last completed film. He seemed to regain his old compulsive enthusiasm for this return to a black-and-white naturalistic study of exploited women. His condition was worsening daily; injections at lunch break were needed to stop the hemorrhaging. But he drove himself and his staff with familiar mercilessness.

Critics were decently receptive to *Street of Shame*, but it came nowhere near Tadashi Imai's treatment of a controversial social issue of

149

the day in his courtroom drama film, *Mahiru no Ankoku* (*Darkness at Noon,* 1956).

Mizoguchi applied a similar manic drive to the beginnings of another project in May of 1956. This was to be *Ōsaka Monogatari* (*The Tale of Osaka*), a film about a miser's tyrannical hold over his family. When Mizoguchi had to be hospitalized without knowing that his case was terminal, shooting was ostensibly postponed for two months. He died on 24 August 1956 at the age of fifty-eight.

Yōkihi (*The Princess Yang Kwei-fei*, 1955)

Based on the famous lyric poem by Po Chü-i, a poet in the T'ang dynasty, *The Princess Yang Kwei-fei* is a conventional melodrama, bringing emperor and kitchen maid together against a background of T'ang dynasty court intrigue. Emperor Hsuan-tsung is the recurring Mizoguchi male prototype: opportunistic and lacking in leadership despite being head of state. After his first wife's death, the emperor distracts himself with musical and artistic pursuits, living with a memory of an empress who he thinks is irreplaceable. He is brought back to life in the ongoing present by the lowly Yu-huan, later renamed Yang Kwei-fei, "lady of the highest rank," by her grateful conquest.

Like any romantic heroine, Yu-huan is portrayed as pure and innocent, in marked contrast to her wicked relatives, who contrive to exploit her position as imperial favorite in order to make the Yang family the first in the land. The story is a familiar one in and out of history. Certainly it offers potential for a study in the interplay of opposing values and the characters who act to widen the breach between them. Yet Mizoguchi's characters are predictable and flat, mere types in a morality play. The political ambition of Yu-huan's elder brother shows itself in a variety of action, most of it having to do with oppressing the masses; however, he never develops beyond a mere cipher of tyranny. Similarly, the emperor remains implausibly passive, a mere stock instance of ruler ruled by a favorite's power-hungry family. His love for the humble Yu-huan does not lead to any broader love of his people, and that, ironically, robs him of her in the end. Yet Mizoguchi fails to develop that irony or any other.

Mizoguchi is interested, rather, in a familiar asset of his heroines: the capacity to draw inner strength out of persecution by a hostile world without; and to make the ultimate sacrifice. The princess Yang Kwei-fei does that. When the people rebel against the excesses of the Yang family and demand her execution, she makes the sacrifice rather than topple her beloved from his throne. The effect is melodramatic, not tragic, since her death is the result of a simplified conflict between good and evil, and because the elements of personal moral dilemma are not there.

Even so, *The Princess Yang Kwei-fei* contains some scenes worthy of

Mizoguchi's genius. The opening sequence, as elsewhere, begins with an unrestricted movement of the camera in a leisurely lateral pan. It moves around the room, traveling across a gauze curtain to reveal Hsuan-tsung, now aged and living in confinement ordered by his son, the present emperor. The free flow of this opening shot creates a strong impression of the ex-emperor's alienation. The flashback begins as he talks about his solitude, addressing a statue of Yang Kwei-fei.

After a blackout, his reminiscences return us to the image of a gauze curtain—this time one of gold. The camera roams through the interior of a palace and moves across this curtain. A breeze moves it slightly. It suggests some court lady's undulating form—the object of the emperor's love. A long shot of a maid yields to a medium shot of a group of musicians behind the curtain. Finally, the curtain, lifted by the wind, reveals the emperor performing with the musicians.[1] Thus we find him in that other form of confinement: bereavement seeking consolation in aesthetic experience. Here, the typical atmosphere of court life is evoked by the fluid camera movement across the curtain.

In the final scene where Emperor Hsuan-tsung, awakened from reverie, is ready to end his days of imprisonment, the recurrent image of the curtain closes the film's circular movement, opening up the possibility of the lovers' final reunion in life after death. Yang Kwei-fei's voice echoes through the room, inviting him to join her, while a returning lateral pan shows the curtain moving subtly, reminiscent of the physical presence of Yang Kwei-fei. This shift in atmosphere does its work; we are convinced by the suggestion that the shift from the elegant, sensual mood of court life (as in the earlier scene with the musicians) to the otherworldliness of this "trembling of the veil" celebrates the lovers' final liberation from the trammels of this world.[2]

The same effect of metamorphosis occurs at the moment of Yang Kwei-fei's surrender of her life. The camera slowly travels along the ground as the robe she has discarded on a tree is wafted gently in the breeze. This image of pulsating warmth and feminine fragility speaks far more eloquently of Yu-huan's fate than would any actual execution scene, which in any case is not shown.

Unfortunately, *The Princess Yang Kwei-fei* is a retreat from the films of the earlier fifties; this work as a whole strikes one as monotonous and insubstantial, a simple story of everlasting love set in surroundings too remote from the director's experience and interest.

Shin Heike Monogatari (New Tales of the Taira Clan, 1955)

Set in the twelfth century, the transition period from an aristocratic to a military regime, *New Tales of the Taira Clan* is a colorful, historical spectacle. One critic characterizes its overall effect as that of "a symphonic drama" in which clashing "tonalities" and contrasting musical scores keep pace with the thematic development of the film.[3] Of course, the less restricted or almost dynamic camera work, which is highlighted by a carefully calculated use of crane and close-ups, contributes to this synthetic effect.

Mizoguchi puts the psychological issues before the sociopolitical ones. Indeed, what holds this spectacular, almost epic film together is the narrative concentration on the educational process of Kiyomori, a young member of the Taira clan who later becomes a charismatic political leader. *New Tales of the Taira Clan* is about his search for identity and self-fulfillment in meaningful action. Mizoguchi shapes the various stages of Kiyomori's spiritual growth, employing those expressive variants which make a "symphonic" rendering possible.

The opening sequence, which consists of eleven shots, introduces us to the historical context of Kiyomori's moral ordeal. Mizoguchi does this deftly, using alternating long and short shots. Even his long single shots fill us in on characters and events with surprising rapidity.

The opening shot, which lasts a few minutes, is one such example. The camera moves diagonally over the capital, Kyoto, then cranes down in the opposite direction to show a huge seething marketplace. As so often happens at the beginning of a Mizoguchi film, the camera browses over the general before settling down to a particular. In this case, it picks out a vendor in the crowd and follows along as he walks to an open road where he stops to read a signboard announcing an imperial decree.

We gather from successive shots of people reading the sign and talking that the country is in a state of siege and countersiege. The government headed by the emperor is opposed, and overruled, by a cabal masterminded by the former (cloistered) emperor. The monks of this country are in open rebellion against the cabal, which wants to divest them of their lands. The cabal is counting on the newly risen samurai class to restore order in the land.

The rest of the sequence clarifies the relation of the Taira clan to these troubles. Tadamori and Kiyomori, father and son, are shown returning from a successful expedition to suppress the rebellion. However, when monks from Mt. Hiei enter the town, carrying the sacred palanquin, even the victorious Taira army must bow to them, kneeling by the roadside.

Clearly, from the outset, Mizoguchi emphasizes humiliation and indignation as the psychological sources of the conflict from which Kiyomori must derive his moral strength. His pride as a samurai is further shattered by the cabal's (cloistered government's) refusal to accord proper reward to the Taira family.

A third and decisive blow to Kiyomori's ego comes when the merchant Banboku leads him to suspect that he is not his father's son. According to

Banboku, Kiyomori's mother, before her marriage to Tadamori, was the mistress of the former emperor Shirakawa. However, when Kiyomori confronts an old family retainer, he is told another story in flashback; according to it, his real father was a monk who was his mother's lover while she was still the emperor's mistress.

Thus, the third stage of Miyomori's moral dilemma brings him face to face with his parents. This scene consists of only three shots, the opening one extremely long and economical. Mizoguchi takes full advantage of the summer arrangement of a samurai household: the partitions have been removed, leaving only pillars to mark off the rooms. This open framed effect lightens the otherwise oppressive emotional intensity of this moment. Tadamori is sitting against a pillar on the left, and his wife, Yasuko, on the right. Kiyomori comes in, places himself between them, and demands to be told who his real father was. Outraged by Kiyomori's request, his mother moves to the next room and stops behind a pillar as the camera pans with her. She is ready, she says, to leave the Taira family for good. Kiyomori approaches and clings to her, but in vain. Yasuko walks off, leaving Kiyomori alone standing against the pillar. Clearly, the pillar serves as a simple yet effective sign of the broken mother-son bond. The rest of the scene unfolds as Tadamori tells Kiyomori that he is his son. Yet Kiyomori thinks that his adoptive father is doing this out of pity for him.

Kiyomori's break with his parents leads him to challenge all parental authority. He feels that he must refuse to become a member of the aristocracy into which his father, Tadamori, has been admitted as a proper reward for his suppression of the monks. He also openly proclaims to the merchant Banboku that he will make his life on his own from now on. However, Mizoguchi brings about a father-son-reconciliation in an ironically dramatic context, since the mother-son breach becomes more decisive. Learning that the court nobles, jealous of Tadamori's success, are plotting his assassination, Kiyomori rushes to the palace grounds to save his father.

Again, Mizoguchi's famous long take returns to the psychologically revealing moment. The scene is a long, bridgelike corridor leading to the ceremonial hall of the palace. Two court nobles and a lady cross it and disappear to the left. A gentleman's drunken voice and a lady's flirtatious laugh merge with the ceremonial music, indicating a strange combination of depravity and decorum—the very mixture of values Kiyomori must reject on his way to maturity.

The stultifying quality associated with the aristocracy is now more fully dramatized when the source of the voices is seen to be Kiyomori's mother (now separated from his father) and the Minister of the Left. They enter the corridor. A low angle shot draws our attention more to their ostentation and equally to Yasuko's coquettishness as they flirt. She even dares to say that her husband now must learn the proper manners of the court. The camera placed on the crane moves up and follows them as they walk along the corridor screen left. Suddenly, the camera is lowered very firmly to ground level to show the face of Kiyomori hiding under the raised floor. His face is full of anger and hatred for all that the aristocracy stands for. Even his costume suggests his decision to rebel: he wears the samurai's armor under his clothes, a notable contrast to the elegant, almost feminine attire of the aristocracy.

This experience, along with Tadamori's suicide, opens up the final discovery of Kiyomori's own lineage. Yasuko reveals to him that his real father was indeed the former emperor Shirakawa. A few close-ups of Kiyomori's face intermittently cut with medium shots of mother and son once more highlight the film's motif: rebellion and humiliation. Instead of rejoicing in his exalted parentage, he declares that he wants to shed every single drop of his father's blood.

Again Kiyomori's repudiation of parental authority must give rise to an independent action, this time publicly. In one of the most dramatically spectacular scenes, the young Kiyomori, fully dressed in a suit of armor, faces a throng of rebellious monks from Mt. Hiei and defies their power. He brings himself to do the unthinkable: commit sacrilege by shooting arrows into the sacred palanquins.

Even so, Mizoguchi clues us into the fact that Kiyomori cannot break free of the fact of his parentage. When he discovers his father's true identity, he is wearing blue and white, colors associated with his mother who is related to the Fujiwara clan (aristocracy). Obviously, this device suggests his links, willy-nilly, with the aristocracy. What remains is to purify his noble blood by taking on the positive attributes which this class has to offer. His marriage to Tokiko, a daughter of an impoverished, yet morally irreproachable branch of the Fujiwara, attests to this. Tokiko, who contrasts in every respect with Yasuko in appearance and sense of values, can act as mother/sister/wife for Kiyomori. She teaches him self-esteem, not self-effacement, together with values like frugality and sincerity. Tadamori has taught the impetuous youth the importance of forbearance and martial strength.

Thus, the film's ending finds Kiyomori a much better man: his moral growth has shown him the way to adequate independence by combining the very best qualities of the aristocratic and military traditions. He has also acquired the kind of wisdom and flexibility it takes to see his mother return to her profession: a dance performer. In the final scene Kiyomori and his party, standing atop a little hill, watch his mother engaging in a leisurely musical pastime together with a group of nobles and dancers.

In contrast to the boisterous market surrounded by walls in the opening sequence, the rising hill covered with young grass is in open frame and evokes an atmosphere of serenity and regeneration appropriate to Kiyomori's fulfillment. The imperial guards chase Kiyomori's party away and the film ends with a close-up (never large) of his determined face while he speaks for the future as he now sees it: "You nobles of the court, enjoy yourselves while you can. Today may be yours; tomorrow belongs to us."

The outstanding artistic achievement of *New Tales of the Taira Clan* is Mizoguchi's emulation of the rhythmic balance which serves as the basis both texturally and thematically. As we have seen, Kiyomori's educational process shifts from rebellion to peace, from impetuosity to maturity. As might be expected, variants of expressive devices, such as colors, imagery, and musical scores (ranging from the traditional Japanese court music to Western adaptations) are used to strike a balance.[4] For example, at Kiyomori's house, the newlyweds, Tokiko and Kiyomori, watch the water led by the bamboo pipe quietly stream into the garden pond. The sound of the water becomes one with the peaceful surroundings of which the couple partake. This signifies the end of Kiyomori's spiritual unrest. The weaving machine Tokiko uses beats in tune with the lyrical music, as she happily weaves Kiyomori's kimono material. There is also the slow graceful dancing of Kiyomori's mother and her companions with the traditional music on the sound track toward the end of the film.

On the other hand, the elements of chaos and discord are illustrated by the cockfights in the market, the rebellious monks gathering around the head instigator, and the dancing at the festival interrupted by the raiding monks. Interestingly, all these incidents are structured around the image of encirclement, while their earlier counterparts have a quality of open framing.

Tonal clash is also found in the scenes depicting Yasuko's promiscuity and Kiyomori's romance respectively. Color motifs, especially red, dominate the screen when Yasuko's affair with a monk is interrupted by the emperor's sudden visit. All the while, there are sounds of sinister orchestral music. Concomitantly, Kiyomori's encounter with Tokiko is shown against a background of the prevailing white along with equally harmonious, lyrical musical scores.

In sum, with its thematic concentration, the polished performance of Raizō Ichikawa (cast as Kiyomori), and the contrasting elements suitable for a specification of the central theme, *New Tales of the Taira Clan*, shows that Mizoguchi has done his best to accommodate himself to this unfamiliar filmic genre.

Akasen Chitai (*Street of Shame*, 1956)

Many critics claim that Mizoguchi's last film, *Street of Shame*, is steeped in realism. This term, in my view, essentially refers to the film's rhetorical attitude rather than its subject—the lives of the women in

Yoshiwara, a licensed pleasure district. Mizoguchi adopts a style of cold detachment and naturalistic observation, discarding the lyrical and sentimental tone which got in his way in the realistic study of prostitutes in *Women of the Night*.

As usual, the central problem of *Street of Shame* is woman's struggle to survive in a male-dominated, money-oriented society. This time, Mizoguchi attaches his theme to a specific political instance: the anti-prostitution law then being debated in the Diet for the fourth time.

From the outset, Mizoguchi deals frankly with the working conditions of women in the pleasure district. The opening sequence (during the credits) shows a birds-eye view of the vicinity of Yoshiwara. The high-angled camera moves along, passing from the ugly roofs of city dwellings to the imposing top of the Honganji Temple. Unlike the war-torn area presented in *Women of the Night*, the city is fully restored and functioning. When the camera finally stops at Yoshiwara, we naturally wonder what kind of values this district has in the rapid modern transformation. The eerie electronic music played during the credits creates a feeling of oppressive emptiness. The district strikes us as a stagnant place, quite out of keeping with all that civilization should imply.[5]

This impression is verified when the old maid of the brothel, perhaps herself once a prostitute, says that in ancient times, the courtesans of Yoshiwara, the center of Edo culture, were highly accomplished in tea-ceremony, flower arrangement, and musical performance. The women we see now are toiling merely to survive. These are common, functional women, with no distinctions of elegance, pride, and talent to dignify their work. Mizoguchi underscores this difference by introducing a series of radio news to show how the antiprostitution law has fared in the Diet during three previous debates; and how the issue, becoming public, has hurt business, so that the prostitute's job has become even more desperate, difficult, and dreary.

In order to provide a total picture of all that the Yoshiwara stands for, Mizoguchi blends together the histories of five such women of different backgrounds, motivations, and value systems. Though they have in common a certain desperate need for money, each stands as a type of oppressed woman. In fact, our sense of them as individuals is subordinate to the case-history aspect of their lives.

The middle-aged Yumeko, widowed, must support a son whom she has left with her in-laws in the country. Her only hope is to let him take care of her after he finishes school.

Yasumi, whose father's embezzlement has caused her downfall, values money above everything. She capitalizes upon her desirability and on her talent as a moneylender as well. She regards prostitution as a means of climbing the social ladder, so that she does her best to accumulate capital for a small respectable business.

For the prostitute Yasumi in Street of Shame, *money is the only means of climbing the social ladder.*

Mickey, once the girl friend of a black soldier, considers her occupation a form of rebellion against her father, a wealthy businessman whose philandering caused her mother great unhappiness.

Yorie, a familiar type of country girl, has volunteered to sell herself to help her poor parents. She dreams of finding someone to love and marry her.

Hanae, a housewife, is burdened with a baby and sick husband. She values survival above respectability.

As the behavior of the owners of the brothel shows too clearly, money is the be-all and end-all of the world of the pleasure district: the only means of survival, and, perhaps, of escape. Not for nothing are the cunning, tight-fisted owners called father and mother by the "girls."

The film involves five episodes, each showing how a hostile environment crushes each woman's dream. The significant exception is the grasping, unprincipled Yasumi. Although each episode exaggerates and cannot, therefore, be taken as a faithful portrayal of the manners and mores of these fallen women, the director's intentions are clear: he wants to achieve a series of dramatically intense effects, giving each actress her due of the lurid limelight. The danger of lapsing into mere melodrama is avoided, thanks to the shifting eye of the camera, which mercilessly exposes the naturalistic forces at work on the lives of these helpless women. They are too much like objects of interest to a pathologist to engage the easy sympathies of an audience bent on having a good cry.

Mickey's encounter with her father, for example, takes place in her room where she mistakes him for what the girls call a "grey-haired romancer." There is continuous cross-cutting between father and daughter taken in close-up. During this we learn of her mother's death caused by the daughter's downfall; of her younger sister's marriage prospects ruined by her profession; and of her father's remarriage. The father begs the daughter to return home, while she reproaches him for taking a second wife so soon. The scene ends when the withdrawing camera shows Mickey seducing her father for money.

Strangely enough, we do not develop any feelings for either, partly because we are surprised at the unusual circumstances, and partly because we reject the values represented by the tyrannical father and rebellious daughter. Thus, the close-ups simply satisfy our intellectual "curiosity" about different emotional phases of the characters; we see how things are, and feel nothing. Thus, Mickey's challenge to paternal authority is achieved only through alienation from all her loved ones. We see how her bid for freedom has left her in a worse situation.

The climax of the episode depicting Yumeko's lapse into insanity after her son casts her off is perhaps overdone, yet the scene leading up to it is a beautiful example of Mizoguchi's skillful control of audience perspective through camera work. As the confrontation scene begins, Yumeko is going to meet her son. A low angle shot of her crossing a slightly raised bridge makes her figure seem much taller, corresponding to her expectations of joy and happiness. Instead, the reunion turns into an occasion for conflict and rejection. The son, ashamed of his mother's profession, asks her not to call him at work because everyone around knows what she is. Yumeko ignores her son's rebuff and moving closer as if to touch him says that it is time he took her in, since she has done so much and is no longer able, because of her age, to maintain herself.

The son refuses outright, claiming that it is the mother's duty to raise the child. Suddenly, the camera singles Yumeko out in close-up. The shot size is not an appeal for our sympathy; rather it invites us to search this thickly madeup face for clues to the rejected mother's emotional response. It remains inscrutable, a mask, leaving events to fill in the picture. Again, the electronic music cues us in with its eerie leitmotiv, signifying decline in the fortunes of women. Thus we are forced to contemplate Yumeko's plight, even as we are not allowed to feel it.

A sentimental undertone creeps into the last long shot. It shows the son hurrying away from his mother (upper left of the screen) while she follows (bottom left screen to the middle) only to be nearly knocked down by a tricycle van. The son does not even look back as the van moves on. The entire event is taken in an extreme long shot from a high angle so that the diminished figure of Yumeko, in contrast to her figure in the opening shot, underscores her dejection. Contrary to the basic filmic grammar of the long shot, the contrast between Yumeko and her uninviting surroundings conveys the felt reality of the poor mother and moves us from feelings of cool neutrality to emotional intensity toward her. At the very end, the sinister electronic music stops suddenly as if the string of a musical instrument had snapped. This is a clear premonition of Yumeko's loss of all hope for the future, which will lead her to madness. (Ironically, in Japanese "Yumeko" means a child with a dream.)

In the scene where Hanae's husband tries to hang himself, we glimpse her strength—a trait shared by most of Mizoguchi's fallen women. A medium shot of her determined face, contrasting with the sobbing husband's head lowered to the floor, offers a moment of detached curiosity about her future. Her protest is uttered against a background of the baby's squalling and the eerie electronic music of the sound track: "How can we call Japan a civilized country when I cannot buy even the baby's milk? I'll live to see how the country fares."

Needless to say, Yorie's brief marriage proves abortive in a world where everything has its price. Freed from one form of bondage, she finds another in marriage to a farmer who considers her a source of cheap labor. Returning to her previous profession, she willingly exchanges one form of loveless slavery for another. The suggestion here is a terrible one: that captive women have no real choice in the matter.

Yasumi's history may offer the last word on this matter of nonchoice, since her career suggests that only a total sell-out, body and soul, will offer the oppressed woman the illusion of escape from her fate. Yet even this escape costs dearly, as Yasumi's unpleasant character shows. She is young, and she is a past mistress of the arts of pleasing and of ruthless manipulation. She saves money, and lends at usurious rates of interest to her fellow prostitutes. Eventually, she buys her freedom, taking over a quilt shop owned by a customer going bankrupt.

However, even a policy of absolute expediency involves high risks. We see this in an attempt on her life by an angry customer who has discovered too late that Yasumi lured him into embezzlement with a false promise of marriage.

Although *Street of Shame* is not a masterpiece, it contains a number of outstanding single shots aimed at offering a carefully, calculated, objective gaze into the lives and feelings of the women of Yoshiwara. As so often is the case with Mizoguchi, shots tend to be long in duration; there are just a few more than 170 in the whole film. The compositional technique is familiar, too: the action takes place in relation to pivotal points in the setting. Here, the entryway and long corridor connecting with stairs leading up to the girls' rooms provide a consistent structure of reference. By employing the long shot, pan, and quite often a deep focus, Mizoguchi moves characters in and out of his chosen frame of reference, so that movement within the shot adds variety and avoids any sense of a "fixed" view. This optical illusion is especially suitable in *Street of Shame*, since it also serves to suggest the hustle and bustle of a pleasure district where human relationships are casual and fleeting against a background of unchanging desperate circumstances.

Mizoguchi also makes deft use of the windowpanes and glass doors in an establishment where the merchandise must importune for itself, and aggressively too. When we see Mickey at the beginning of the film, we are inside the brothel looking through a large window while she solicits outside. Then she comes inside to strike a pose in a gaudy outsize scallop shell, calling herself Venus. She is, of course, a goddess for hire, so when a man is seen passing by the window, she hurries back outside where we see her accosting him. Time and again these through-the-glass doublings of the view offered by a long shot enrich the action of a scene and obviate the need for many cuts.

Mizoguchi's camera can be powerfully expressive in subtle ways, even when it is trained with a mercilessly observant eye on the seamy side of life. In one such scene, Hanae with her husband and baby enters a small eating place to order noodles, the cheapest item on the menu. A series of reverse-angle shots studies the squalid marks of poverty on these people and their surroundings. The husband, viewed from the back, exhibits the posture of a man bowed and broken by the weight of a commonplace destiny. The camera moves to Hanae's back, or rather the back of her overcoat, an obvious hand-me-down too large and too long, a garment that says much about the life of this poverty-stricken couple.

The final single shot is the most revealing of her plight as the prostitute/mother/wife. It is a front shot of Hanae holding the baby with her legs slightly apart—an impossible way of sitting among decent women. Moreover, in place of the shoes she cannot possibly afford, she wears Japanese vinyl sandals along with Western stockings. The camera's low angle emphasizes the bulky and unattractive legs, which are still her stock in trade. Her eyes behind the equally unattractive glasses are lusterless. Hanae is the very image of the woman who, though deprived of zest and hope for life, still holds on to life with desperate persistence. No wonder the proprietess remarks earlier that Hanae looks too much like a housewife to bring in many customers.

Despite her misfortunes, Hanae is still capable of showing affection for her feckless, woebegone spouse. Hungry as she is, she offers him her bowl of noodles; and he empties it greedily.

An obvious, but effective coda brings the story of the women of the pleasure district full circle. It begins with a dissolve from the close-up of Shizuko, a little girl from a coal mining village, into a focus on her face being made up by the madame of the brothel. The contrast is all the stronger for our having seen this country girl wolf down some take-out food, saying that she has never eaten such a tasty dish. Now the brothel maid observes in a matter-of-fact tone of voice that the little virgin is pretty to look at. Already we know what is to follow.

A long shot shows Mickey and this neophyte, Shizuko, standing outside the brothel entrance. Shizuko, all dolled up in a kimono, is studied in a full-length shot which draws our attention to her nervous fidgeting. Mickey is perfectly at ease in her gaudy Western dress. She tells Shizuko to chuck her virginity straightaway and adds that she will teach her how.

Another long shot shows the two soliciting together. They blend in so well with the setting that we get the feeling that they are part and parcel of this nighttime life, and the genuine playthings of unkind fate.

The camera follows and records the progress of Shizuko's apprenticeship in newsreel fashion. One close-up captures just half of her figure as she hides behind the front door, calling out awkwardly to a customer, "Please, come in." Another close-up of her face alone repeats this awkward solicitation.[6] Shizuko's face is an open book; shyness, shame, and resignation are written there, along with fear. The camera takes in a

notice above the brothel door: "Member of the Proprietors' Association." The crowning irony is supplied by the earlier newscast announcing the failure of the Diet to pass an antiprostitution law: so much for the
fourth attempt at legal remedy.

Unfortunately, Mizoguchi overplays the final moment of the film.
Realistic perspective here yields to sentimental compromise. Shizuko's
face disappears behind the brothel wall, clearly indicating her lack of
nerve for her first night. Yet the fade which ends the picture on this note
is too easy—too familiar a device for elegizing the fate of yet another
woman trapped by life. The sinister electronic music returns to the
sound track for an effect of fatalistic circularity. First and last and always,
Mizoguchi seems to have been convinced that the tragedy of one woman
would inevitably be followed by that of another.

11

Conclusion: On a More Personal Note

STRICTLY SPEAKING, it is not the critic's task to account for a personal bias, but I think it is appropriate to the praise and evaluation of Mizoguchi's art to explain why his films have stimulated and delighted me so much. As a native Japanese, I find that this director's presence behind the camera revivifies the cultural climate of my country in a peculiarly rich way. His vision is keenly observant and so expressive in subtle ways that the native viewer experiences a shock of recognition and of admiration for everyday nuances used with such art. Perhaps this is especially the case with those like myself, born and raised in the Kansai area where Mizoguchi's finest films, with one exception (*The Straits of Love and Hate*), were made and also set. We see how he has captured the mood of a character in the peculiar stillness centered in the back of a woman moving away from the camera; or in some slight shift in the intonation of the slow, rhythmical Kansai dialect. In this sense, I think of Mizoguchi's films as being more challenging to my "sense of the Japanese" than, say, those of Kurosawa and Ozu, who range over places less native to me.

Naturally, I have tried to give cultural specifics their due in this book, whose method of analysis follows several critical approaches. Like any "auteuriste," I have tried to identify recurring thematic and stylistic traits which can be considered characteristic of this director and which illuminate his art. Like any structuralist, I have tried to de-compose various works in order to see how they were achieved. And, of course, I have taken into account some aspects of the life and personality of this complex and often contradictory man.

In general, I have shied away from any strongly ideological commitment as being foreign to Mizoguchi's aims and achievements. Despite his obvious fixation on the sacrificial woman, he is not a moralist with a social critique to offer, much less a vision of a better human life. Rather, as he himself once said, his posture is that of a dedicated observer and recorder: "In the contemporary genre film, I must portray life as it is

165

lived by people. That is all."[1] We have seen how badly he could do when wartime censors put ideological commitments between him and his art.

On the whole, Mizoguchi was a solitary, eccentric figure. Though traditionalist to the core, he remained aloof from the mainstream of Japanese filmmaking. He was forever searching for new modes of representation. This led to his wide-ranging, sometimes ill-advised, experiments. In all things and sometimes calamitously, he was a perfectionist, driving himself and others as only a perfectionist would dream of doing.

His finest works have been influential in both East and West. The so-called French "New Wave" directors, for example, have been especially attentive. Jean-Luc Godard is said to have seen *The Life of Oharu* more than ten times. Like many Westerners, he has noticed that Mizoguchi's moving camera creates effects of lightning similar to the touch Hokusai brings to his *ukiyoe* prints. It is pleasantly ironic that the French New Wave returned Mizoguchi to Japan, influencing her own New Wave directors of the early sixties.

Sad to say, Mizoguchi has found imitators, but no equals in his country. Perhaps the most noteworthy follower in Mizoguchi's footsteps is Kirirō Urayama, a director of *Kyūpora no Aru Machi (The Town with a Cupola)* and *Watashi no Suteta Onna (The Woman I Left Behind)*. Certainly he has learned that a director must develop the talents of the actresses who come his way.

Few directors anywhere can have brought such a degree of dedication to their art as Mizoguchi. His cultural authenticity, "diabolical" drive, paradoxical personality, and profound vision of human existence combined to make Mizoguchi a major figure in the Japanese film industry. As his films become more familiar in the West and East, I hope that this book, and others like it, will help audiences see more deeply into the rich complexities of Mizoguchi's art.

Notes and References

Preface

1. Kaneto Shindō's recent book, *Aru Eiga Kantoku: Mizoguchi Kenji to Nihon Eiga* (A film director: Kenji Mizoguchi and Japanese film) (Tokyo, 1976), along with his film, *Aru Eiga Kantoku no Shōgai (Kenji Mizoguchi: The Life of a Film Director*, 1975), is most revealing of the crucial incidents in his career, which most affected Mizoguchi both as a director and as a man. Yoshikata Yoda's *Mizoguchi Kenji no Hito to Geijutsu* (Kenji Mizoguchi: the man and his life) (Tokyo, 1970) is equally evocative of Mizoguchi's life and its relationship with his art.
2. Hideo Tsumura, *Mizoguchi Kenji to Iu Onoko* (A man called Kenji Mizoguchi) (Tokyo, 1977), pp. 146–47.
3. Yoda, *Mizoguchi Kenji no Hito to Geijutsu*, p. 12.

Chapter One

1. Shindō, *Aru Eiga Kantoku*, p. 110.
2. Ibid., p. 112.
3. Only a twenty-minute incomplete print is available now.
4. Masotoshi Ōba et al. *Film Center: Mizoguchi Kenji Tokushū* (Special issue on Kenji Mizoguchi), no. 48 (Tokyo, 1978), p. 10.
5. Yoda, *Mizoguchi Kenji no Hito to Geijutsu*, p. 111.

Chapter Two

1. Shindō, *Aru Eiga Kantoku*, p. 116.
2. Ibid., p. 121.
3. There are three versions of *White Threads of the Cascade* available today. The first version, in the possession of the Film Center of the Tokyo Museum of Modern Art, does not contain Shiraito's dream (in prison) in which she envisions herself smilingly watching carp, a symbol of rising fortune, swimming in a pond, while thinking of her happy reunion with Kinya. It also lacks the final scene of Kinya's suicide, ending in his writing of a letter of resignation. The second version, which was cut during the Allied Occupation, has a happy

ending. The sections of Kinya's sentencing Shiraito and his subsequent suicide are deleted, and the dream scene are added to the end. The third and most complete version, which I saw at the Bungeiza Theater in Tokyo, has both the dream and the suicide scenes. I used the last version for my analysis.

4. Quoted by Yoda in *Mizoguchi Kenji no Hito to Geijutsu*, p. 41.

5. Shindō, *Aru Eiga Kantoku*, p. 125.

6. "Mizoguchi Kenji," in *Nihon Eiga Sakka Ron* (On Japanese filmmakers) (Tokyo, 1936), p. 207.

7. In the original, however, Fujio meets sudden death.

8. Though Fujio has an elder stepbrother, he refuses to inherit the family name, allowing her to take this responsibility.

9. Noël Burch, *To the Distant Observer: Form and Meaning in the Japanese Cinema* (Berkeley, 1979), pp. 223–24. Burch claims that *Poppy* demonstrates Mizoguchi's radical break with "what already appeared to be the main thrust of Mizoguchi's developing stylistics." While the fixed camera position indicates his Japanese style, "reverse-field figures and medium close-ups abound" constitute the Western mode of representation.

Chapter Three

1. For example, Kazuo Yamada claims that Mizoguchi's realism in *Sisters of the Gion* and *Osaka Elegy* encompasses the two different trends evident in his earlier films: the social criticism of *The Metropolitan Symphony* (1929), and the insight into female psychology of *Nihonbashi* (1929) and *White Threads of the Cascade* (1933); see *Nihon Eiga no Hachijūnen* (Eighty years of Japanese Cinema) (Tokyo: Isseisha, 1976), p. 92. Yasuzō Masumura, film director and critic, considers Mizoguchi's realism distinctly different from Western realism represented by Stroheim. Masumura argues that the reality created in Mizoguchi's films is not a faithful rendition of our daily reality but a fabricated reality of universal feelings among the Japanese; see "Watashi no Eiga Shūgyō: 5. Mizoguchi ni Okeru Riarizumu" (My film apprenticeship: 5. Realism in Mizoguchi), *Kinema Junpō*, no. 449 (September 1967):78–80.

2. Quoted in Motohiko Fujita, *Nihon Eiga Gendaishi: Shōwa Jūnendai* (The contemporary history of Japanese cinema: 1935–1945) (Tokyo, 1977), p. 114.

3. Kenji Mizoguchi, "Tsuchi no Nioi: *Gion no Shimai* o Tsukuru Mae ni" (The smell of the earth: before making *Sisters of the Gion*), *Kinema Junpō*, no. 582 (July 1936):60–61.

4. Ibid., p. 60.

5. Fujita, *Nihon Eiga Gendaishi*, p. 114.

6. Donald Richie, *Japanese Cinema: Film Style and National Character* (Garden City, N.Y., 1971), pp. xix–xx.

7. Burch, *To the Distant Observer*, pp. 218–19.

8. "Mizoguchi Kenji Zadankai" (Round table discussion with Mizoguchi), *Kinema Junpō*, no. 597 (January 1937):258.

9. Yoshikata Yoda, "Mizoguchi Kenji no Sobyō" (A rough sketch of Kenji Mizoguchi), *Kinema Junpō*, no. 597 (January 1937):187.

10. Mizoguchi, "Tsuchi no Nioi," p. 60.

11. In the original script, there is a scene which reveals man's egoism. On a train bound for his home town, Furusawa celebrates his future with Sadakichi, his ex-employee. Asked by Sadakichi what he is going to do with Umekichi, he cheerfully replies that he will send her a final payment. He adds that after all a geisha like her is only after money.

12. Dudley Andrew and Paul Andrew, *Kenji Mizoguchi: A Guide to References and Resources* (Boston, 1981), p. 29.

Chapter Four

1. Tadao Satō, *Mizoguchi Kenji no Sekai* (The world of Kenji Mizoguchi) (Tokyo, 1982), p. 62.

2. Yoshikata Yoda, "Joyūtsukuri no Meijin: Mizoguchi Enshutsu no Himitsu" (A great trainer of actresses: the secret of Mizoguchi's directing), *Geijutsu Shinchō*, November 1956, p. 165.

3. Satō, *Mizoguchi Kenji no Sekai*, p. 62.

Chapter Five

1. Kenji Mizoguchi, "*Genroku Chūshingura* no Konpon Taido" (My fundamental attitude behind *The Loyal 47 Ronin*), *Jidai Eiga* 18 (September 1941):60.

2. Shindō, *Aru Eiga Kantoku*, p. 145.

3. According to Satō, *Mizoguchi Kenji no Sekai*, p. 253, Mizoguchi's decision to exclude the scene of the retainers' attack on Kira's mansion, the greatest "spectacle" offered by other versions, can be attributed to his adherence to realism. Realistic choreography for swordfighting—as opposed to ritualistic—had not yet been perfected in Japanese cinema studios. Mizoguchi thought that his faithful portrayal of samurai life would be marred by the mannered fighting available to him.

4. Ibid., pp. 250–51.

5. Ōba, p. 21.

Chapter Six

1. Shindō, *Aru Eiga Kantoku*, p. 161.

2. Yoda, *Mizoguchi Kenji no Hito to Geijutsu*, p. 131.

3. Satō, *Mizoguchi Kenji no Sekai*, p. 159.

4. Junichirō Tanaka, *Nihon Eiga Hattatsushi: Sengo Eiga no Kaihō* (History of the development of Japanese film: liberation in postwar films) (Tokyo: Chūō Kōron, 1976), 3:215–16.

5. Shindō, *Aru Eiga Kantoku*, p. 161.

6. Yoda, *Mizoguchi Kenji no Hito to Geijutsu*, pp. 146–47.

Chapter Seven

1. Yoda, *Mizoguchi Kenji no Hito to Geijutsu*, p. 178.

2. Jūzaburō Futaba, "*Oyūsama*" (*Miss Oyū*), *Kinema Junpō*, no. 19 (July 1951):37.

3. Tadao Satō, "*Yuki Fujin Ezu*: Mizoguchi Narusawa Ryōsakuhin no Hikaku" (*A Picture of Madame Yuki*: a comparison of Mizoguchi's and Narusawa's works), *Shinario* 31 (May 1975):97–99.
4. David Owen, *Mizoguchi: The Master* (New York, 1981), p. 134.
5. For a detailed analysis of Mizoguchi's adaptation of Tanizaki's novella and also his use of the technique of scroll painting, see Dudley Andrew, "Passion and Pictorialism in Mizoguchi's *Miss Oyū*, " presented at the Association for Asian Studies Conference, Chicago, 3 April 1982.
6. Yoda, *Mizoguchi Kenji no Hito to Geijutsu*, pp. 184–87.

Chapter Eight

1. Shindō, *Aru Eiga Kantoku*, pp. 196–97.
2. For a comparative study of the original and its film version, see Satō, *Mizoguchi Kenji no Sekai*, pp. 180–90.
3. Jonathan Rosenbaum, "*Saikaku Ichidai Onna*" (*The Life of Oharu*), *Monthly Film Bulletin* 42, no. 494 (March 1975):66.
4. This technique is pointed out by a number of critics. For example, see Joan Mellen, *The Waves at Genji's Door: Japan Through Its Cinema* (New York, 1976), pp. 260–61.
5. Satō, *Mizoguchi Kenji no Sekai*, pp. 192–93.
6. Ibid., pp. 191–92.
7. Kazuo Kawabe, et al., "Zadankai: *Saikaku Ichidai Onna* ga Teiki Suro Mono" (Round table discussion: what *The Life of Oharu* has to offer), *Shinario* 23 (June 1967):16.
8. Rosenbaum, "*Saikaku Ichidai Onna*," p. 66.
9. Yoda, *Mizoguchi Kenji no Hito to Geijutsu*, p. 216.
10. For an insightful treatment of the long panorama which opens and closes *Ugetsu*, see Donald Richie, "Kenji Mizoguchi," in *Cinema: A Critical Study*, ed. Richard Roud (London, 1980), p. 702.
11. Audie Bock, *Japanese Film Directors* (Tokyo, 1978), p. 49.
12. Mellen, *The Waves*, pp. 103–4.
13. Bock, *Japanese Film Directors*, p. 49.

Chapter Nine

1. Heiichi Sugiyama, "*Gion Bayashi*" (*Gion Festival Music*), *Eiga Hyōron* 10 (October 1953):76–78.
2. Sugiyama suggests that the old maid watching the domestic scene stands for the attitudes of the director, who remains emotionally uninvolved as the drama unfolds. See ibid., p. 77.
3. Mizoguchi altered the original short story by Ōgai Mori to suit the motif of human suffering. For example, in the original, the mother recovers from blindness when she touches the statue of the goddess of mercy. Sanshō's estate is not destroyed by the liberated slaves who seek revenge, but prospers after they are settled on it as tenants. For an extensive comparison of Ōgai's short story, Mizoguchi's film version, and the folklore which inspired Ōgai's work, see Satō,

Mizoguchi Kenji no Sekai, p. 204–15. For a study of Mizoguchi's adaptation of Ōgai's work, see also Hajime Takizawa, "*Sanshō Dayū*" (*Sanshō the Bailiff*), *Eiga Hyōron* 11 (May 1954):69–70, and Shinbi Iida, "*Sanshō Dayū*: Gensaku to Eiga" (*Sanshō the Bailiff*: the original and the film), *Eiga Geijutsu* 9, no. 1 (1954):52–55.

4. John Belton, "The Crucified Lovers of Mizoguchi," *Film Quarterly* 25 (Fall 1971):16. Belton argues that confinement becomes not only "a social and political metaphor" but an artistic one as well.

5. For a fuller treatment of Mizoguchi's awareness of a character's vertical movement as expressive of psychology, see Satō, "Mizoguchi Kenji no Ue to Shita" (The "highs" and the "lows" in Kenji Mizoguchi's films), *Kikan Eizō* 1 (May 1975):43–52 (in *Mizoguchi Kenji no Sekai,* pp. 284–88, 296–305).

6. Belton points out that this "slow, clockwise movement of the boat" metaphorically defines "wordlessly the transcendent quality of the lovers' relationship" ("The Crucified Lovers," p. 19).

7. Satō, *Mizoguchi Kenji no Sekai,* pp. 301–2.

Chapter Ten

1. Joseph Anderson and Donald Richie state that the opening scene where the camera wanders through the halls of the palace and finally captures the gauze curtain is a superb example of Mizoguchi's controlled camera movement." See Anderson and Richie, "Kenji Mizoguchi," *Sight and Sound* 25 (Autumn 1955):81.

2. Mellen claims that the finale reveals "Mizoguchi meeting the moment of his own death, and welcoming his departure from a world that has offered only grief to woman—and to man as well." (*The Waves,* p. 269).

3. Michael McKegney, "*New Tales of the Taira Clan (Shin Heike Monogatari),*" *Village Voice,* 5 August 1971, p. 51.

4. Ibid. McKegney points out that dichotomous elements such as "the chaos of the crowded streets and the serene symmetry of the imperial court, the winter of despair and the spring of hope," and "conflict and repose" are "ultimately contained in the balance of Nature's order."

5. The critic Masuo Yamauchi points out that this electronic music is an apt method for creating the impression of Yoshiwara's being left out of the progress of modernization. See Masuo Yamauchi, "*Akasen Chitai* to Kyakkanteki Byōsha" (*Street of Shame* and objective description), *Eiga Hyōron* 13 (June 1956):78.

6. Yasuhiko Ōhashi, "*Akasen Chitai*: Sono Engi" (Acting in *Street of Shame*), *Eiga Geijutsu* 4, no. 5 (1956):70. Ōhashi argues that a several-second shot of Shizuko accosting a customer superbly condenses the motif of the film.

Chapter Eleven

1. Kenji Mizoguchi et al., "Mizoguchi Kenji Zadankai" (A roundtable discussion with Kenji Mizoguchi), *Kinema Junpō,* no. 597 (January 1937):260.

Selected Bibliography

Primary Sources

1. Articles

"Tsuchi no Nioi: *Gion no Shimai* o Tsukuru Mae ni" (The smell of the earth: before making *Sisters of the Gion*). *Kinema Junpō*, no. 582 (July 1936):60–61. Mizoguchi describes his attempt to depict the earthiness of Osakaites and Kyotoites in *Osaka Elegy* and *Sisters of the Gion* respectively.

2. Interviews

"Enshutsu Izen" (Before directing). Interview with Mizoguchi by Hajime Takizawa. *Eiga Hyōron* 12 (December 1955):27–29. Mizoguchi talks about his camera work, concern with costumes and props, and interest in literary adaptations.

"Mizoguchi Kenji Zadankai" (Round-table discussion with Kenji Mizoguchi). *Kinema Junpō*, no. 597 (January 1937):255–62. Interview with Mizoguchi by Fuyuhiko Kitagawa et al. Topics discussed include Mizoguchi's reason for filming *Osaka Elegy,* his interest in art, favorite female types, and social consciousness as artist, etc.

Secondary Sources

1. Bibliography

Andrew, Dudley, and Andrew, Paul. *Kanji Mizoguchi: A Guide to References and Resources.* Boston: G. K. Hall, 1981. A comprehensive, up-to-date bibliography of materials in English, Japanese, and some European languages, along with a filmography, plot synopses, and a critical introduction to Mizoguchi's biography, style, and the literary sources of his films.

2. Books and parts of books

Bock, Audie. "Kenji Mizoguchi, 1898–1956." In *Japanese Film Directors.* Tokyo: Kodansha International, 1978, pp. 33–68. A concise but illuminating survey of Mizoguchi's life, feminism, and films, especially *Ugetsu.* This chapter also includes a filmography with short plot summaries.

Burch, Noël. "Mizoguchi Kenji." In *To the Distant Observer: Form and Meaning in the Japanese Cinema.* Berkeley: University of California Press, 1979, pp. 217–46. An ambitious semiotic approach to Mizoguchi's mode of representation, focusing on his films of the late thirties and early forties.

Fujita, Motohiko. "Josei Gyōshi no Me to Shindo: Mizoguchi Kenji no Riarizumu" (Depth of scrutiny of women: Kenji Mizoguchi's realism). In *Nihon Eiga Gendaishi: Shōwa Jūnendai* (The contemporary history of Japanese Cinema: 1934–1945). Tokyo: Kashinsha, 1977, pp. 103–32. A biographical, historical, and contextual approach to Mizoguchi's realism as revealed in representative films made between 1926 and 1941.

Iijima, Tadashi. "Mizoguchi Kenji." In *Nihon Eigashi* (History of Japanese Cinema). Tokyo: Hakusuisha, 1955, pp. 219–40. A survey of Mizoguchi's early filmmaking in three phases: silent films (1933–34), realism (1936–38), and aestheticism (1931–41).

Mellen, Joan. *The Waves at Genji's Door: Japan Through Its Cinema*. New York: Pantheon, 1976. Various sections contain insightful analyses of Mizoguchi's films about women from a feminist perspective.

Murakami, Tadahisa. "Mizoguchi Kenji." In *Nihon Eiga Sakka Ron* (On Japanese filmmakers). Tokyo: Kinema Junpō, 1936, pp. 201–16. Traces Mizoguchi's filmmaking career from 1923 to 1935, concentrating on *Gion Festival*, *The Mountain Pass of Love and Hate*, and *The Downfall of Osen*.

Ōba, Masatoshi et al. *Film Center: Mizoguchi Kenji Tokushū* (Special issue on Kenji Mizoguchi), no. 48. Tokyo: Film Center, 1978. A critical explication of Mizoguchi's extant films, along with synopses. It also contains a critical introduction to Mizoguchi's filmmaking along with a filmography.

Owen, David. *Mizoguchi: The Master*. New York: Japan Society, 1981. Concise yet useful reviews of Mizoguchi's thirty films shown at the Japan Film Center, New York, along with brief introductions by Dudley Andrew and Peter Grilli.

Richie, Donald. "Kenji Mizoguchi." In *Cinema: A Critical Study*. Vol. 2. Edited by Richard Roud. London: Secker & Warburg, 1980, pp. 693–703. One of the most illuminating evaluations of Mizoguchi's subject, style, and accomplishments as a director.

———. *Japanese Cinema: Film Style and National Character*. Garden City, N.Y.: Anchor Books, 1971. Contains a cogent survey of Mizoguchi's themes relating to women, along with analyses of his methods, camera work especially, as revealed in a number of representative films.

Satō, Tadao. *Mizoguchi Kenji no Sekai* (The world of Kenji Mizoguchi). Tokyo: Chikuma Shobō, 1982. A comprehensive and insightful study of Mizoguchi's early years at Nikkatsu studios, his involvement in the *shinpa* stage, his camera work, and his exploration of subjects relating to women. This study covers almost all of his major works.

———. "Kenji Mizoguchi." In *Nihon Eiga no Kyoshōtatchi* (Masters of Japanese film). Tokyo: Gakuyō Shobō, 1979, pp. 81–89. Satō traces the development of Mizoguchi's consistent preoccupation with the theme of a woman's sacrifice.

Shindō, Kaneto. *Aru Eiga Kantoku: Mizoguchi Kenji to Nihon Eiga*. (A film director: Kenji Mizoguchi and Japanese film). Tokyo: Iwanami Shoten, 1976. A personal biography of Mizoguchi incorporating talks by those who worked closely with him.

Tsumura, Hideo. *Mizoguchi Kenji to Iu Onoko* (A man called Kenji Mizoguchi). Tokyo: Haga Shoten, 1977. Chiefly a collection of humorous yet lucid anecdotes focusing on Mizoguchi's idiosyncrasies. Also contains a chapter on Kinuyo Tanaka's relationship with Mizoguchi along with a filmography and chronology.

Yoda, Yoshikata. *Mizoguchi Kenji no Hito to Geijutsu* (Kenji Mizoguchi: The man and his art). Tokyo: Tabata Shoten, 1970. A personal yet comprehensive biography of Mizoguchi, by the writer of many screenplays for his films, describing the circumstances related to his filmmaking along with various anecdotes. From time to time Yoda offers sensitive observations on Mizoguchi's stylistic development.

3. Articles

Anderson, Joseph, and Richie, Donald. "Kenji Mizoguchi." *Sight and Sound* 25 (Autumn 1955):76–81. A concise chronological survey of Mizoguchi's life, art, and films. One of the earliest essays on Mizoguchi to appear in English.

Belton, John. "The Crucified Lovers of Mizoguchi." *Film Quarterly* 25 (Fall 1971):15–19. This article on *The Crucified Lovers* offers good insight into Mizoguchi's style, especially as it relates to the film's narrative development.

Iida, Shinbi. "*Sanshō Dayū*: Gensaku to Eiga" (*Sanshō the Bailiff*: the original and the film). *Eiga Geijutsu* 9, no. 1 (1954):52–55. Comparing the film with Ōgai's original, Iida points out that Mizoguchi's addition of the subplot dealing with the sufferings of both the masses and women adds greater pathos to the film.

Iwasaki, Akira. "Mizoguchi Kenji no Riarizumu" (Kenji Mizoguchi's realism). *Kinema Junpō*, no. 294 (September 1961):56–58. Iwasaki claims that the realism revealed in *Osaka Elegy* and *Sisters of the Gion* forms the backbone of Mizoguchi's technique, though this realism continues to be modified in his later works.

Kawabe, Kazuo et al. "Zadankai: *Saikaku Ichidai Onna* ga Teiki Suru Mono" (Round-table discussion: What *The Life of Oharu* has to offer) *Shinario* 23 (June 1967):14–26. A number of directors and a scenarist discuss Mizoguchi's characterization of Oharu, the film's world view, and his influence on the French New Wave directors.

McDonald, Keiko. "Form and Function in *Osaka Elegy*." *Film Criticism* 6, no. 2 (Winter 1982):35–44. An analysis of the film's thematic development, style, and their combined effect on the viewer's point of view.

McKegney, Michael. "*New Tales of the Taira Clan* (*Shin Heike Monogatari*)." *Village Voice*, 5 August 1971. p. 51. Includes a cogent analysis of a clash of tonalities which contributes to the film's narrative concentration.

Masumura, Yasuzō. "Watashi no Eiga Shūgyō: 5. Mizoguchi ni Okeru Riarizumu" (My film apprenticeship: 5. Realism in Mizoguchi). *Kinema Junpō*, no. 449 (September 1967):78–80. Includes a discussion of the resemblance of Mizoguchi's realism to that of Von Stroheim, with particular reference to their use of sets.

Mitsui, Yōtarō. "*Akasen Chitai*" (*Street of Shame*). *Eiga Hyōron* 13 (April 1956):67–69. A review of *Street of Shame* with focus on several episodes.

Rosenbaum, Jonathan. *"Saikaku Ichidai Onna (The Life of Oharu)."* *Monthly Film Bulletin* 42, no. 494 (March 1975):66. Evaluates the film as a "powerful feminist protest."

Satō, Tadao. "Mizoguchi Kenji no Geijutsu" (The art of Kenji Mizoguchi). *Shinario* 30 (December 1974):106–11. A biographical approach to the motif of a woman's sacrifice in terms of the sudden madness of Mizoguchi's wife. It also contains a detailed critical analysis of *The Downwall of Osen*.

————. "Mizoguchi Kenji no Ue to Shita" (The highs and lows in Kenji Mizoguchi's films). *Kikan Eizō* 1 (May 1975):42–45. Reprinted in *Mizoguchi Kenji no Sekai* (The World of Kenji Mizoguchi), pp. 284–88, 296–305. A perceptive analysis of Mizoguchi's use of camera angle and vertical movement of characters to achieve thematic effects.

————. *"Yuki Fujin Ezu*: Mizoguchi Narusawa Ryōsakuhin no Hikaku" (A Picture of Madame Yuki: a Comparison of Mizoguch's and Narusawa's works). *Shinario* 31 (May 1975):96–99. A comparison of the two film versions in characterization, plot, and setting.

Sugiyama, Heiichi. *"Gion Bayashi" (Gion Festival Music)*. *Eiga Hyōron* 10 (October 1953):76–78. Describes Mizoguchi's sensitivity to the manners of people in the Gion as well as sound effects.

Yamauchi, Masuo. *"Akasen Chitai* to Kyakkanteki Byōsha" (*Street of Shame* and objective depiction). *Eiga Hyōron* 13 (June 1956):78–80. This article is chiefly concerned with Mizoguchi's treatment of different social problems related to prostitution.

Filmography

THIS FILMOGRAPHY covers only the extant films (indicated by an asterisk) with a mere listing of the titles of the lost ones. For a more complete filmography, see Dudley Andrew and Paul Andrew, *Kenji Mizoguchi: A Guide to References and Resources* (Boston: G. K. Hall, 1981).

Silent Films

THE RESURRECTION OF LOVE (*Ai ni Yomigaeru Hi*, 1923)
HOMETOWN (*Kokyō*, 1923)
THE DREAM PATH OF YOUTH (*Seishun no Yumeji*, 1923)
CITY OF DESIRE (*Joen no Chimata*, 1923)
FAILURE'S SONG IS SAD (*Haizan no Uta wa Kanashi*, 1923)
813: THE ADVENTURE OF ARSÈNE LUPIN (*813*, 1923)
FOGGY HARBOR (*Kiri no Minato*, 1923)
IN THE RUINS (*Haikyo no Naka*, 1923)
THE NIGHT (*Yoru*, 1923)
BLOOD AND SOUL (*Chi to Rei*, 1923)
THE SONG OF THE MOUNTAIN PASS (*Tōge no Uta*, 1923)
THE SAD IDIOT (*Kanashiki Hakuchi*, 1924)
DEATH AT DAWN (*Akatsuki no Shi*, 1924)
THE QUEEN OF MODERN TIMES (*Gendai no Joō*, 1924)
WOMEN ARE STRONG (*Josei wa Tsuyoshi*, 1924)
THIS DUSTY WORLD (*Jinkyō*, 1924)
TURKEYS IN A ROW (*Shichimenchō no Yukue*, 1924)
A CHRONICLE OF MAY RAIN (*Samidare Zōshi*, 1924)
A WOMAN OF PLEASURE (*Kannaku no Onna*, 1924)
QUEEN OF THE CIRCUS (*Kyokubadan no Joō*, 1924)
NO MONEY, NO FIGHT (*Musen Fusen*, 1925)
OUT OF COLLEGE (*Gakusō o Idete*, 1925)
THE EARTH SMILES (*Daichi was Hohoemu*, 1925)
THE WHITE LILY LAMENTS (*Shirayuri wa Nageku*, 1925)
SHINING IN THE RED SUNSET (*Akai Yūhi ni Terasarete*, 1925)
STREET SKETCHES (*Gaijō no Suketchi*, 1925)
THE HUMAN BEING (*Ningen*, 1925)

*THE SONG OF HOME (*Furusato no Uta*) (Nikkatsu Taishōgun, 1925)
Screenplay: Ryūnosuke Shimizu
Photography: Tatsuyuki Yokota
Cast: Shigeru Kido (Naotarō Takeda), Masujirō Tagaki (Naotarō's father), Sueko Itō (Naotarō's mother)
Running Time: 45 minutes
Premiere: 3 December 1925
Rental: Not in distribution
GENERAL NOGI AND KUMASAN (*Nogi Taishō to Kumasan*, 1925)
THE COPPER COIN KING (*Dōka-ō*, 1926)
A PAPER DOLL'S WHISPER OF SPRING (*Kaminingyō Haru no Sasayaki*, 1926)
MY FAULT, NEW VERSION (*Shin Ono ga Tsumi*, 1926)
THE PASSION OF A WOMAN TEACHER (*Kyōren no Onna Shishō*, 1926)
THE BOY OF THE SEA (*Kaikoku Danji*, 1926)
MONEY (*Kane*, 1926)
THE IMPERIAL GRACE (*Kōon*, 1927)
THE CUCKOO (*Jihi Shinchō*, 1927)
A MAN'S LIFE (*Hito no Isshō*, 1928)
MY LOVELY DAUGHTER (*Musume Kawaiya*, 1928)
NIHONBASHI (*Nihonbashi*, 1929)
THE MORNING SUN SHINES (*Asahi wa Kagayaku*, 1929)
*TOKYO MARCH (Tōkyō Kōshinkyoku) (Nikkatsu Uzumasa, 1929)
Screenplay: Chiio Kimura and Shūichi Hatamoto
Photography: Tatsuyuki Yokota
Cast: Shizue Natsukawa (Orie), Takako Irie (Sayuriko)
Premiere: 31 May 1929
Only incomplete print extant; not available for rent or sale.
METROPOLITAN SYMPHONY (*Tokai Kōkyōgaku*, 1929)

Transitional Period
*HOME TOWN (*Furusato*) (Nikkatsu Uzumasa, 1930, sound)
Screenplay: Satoshi Kisaragi, Shūichi Hatamoto and Masashi Kobayashi
Photography: Tatsuyuki Yokota and Yoshio Mineo
Music: Toyoaki Tanaka
Cast: Yoshie Fujiwara (Fujimura), Shizue Natsukawa (Ayako)
Running Time: 107 minutes
Premiere: 14 March 1930
Rental: Not in distribution
MISTRESS OF A FOREIGNER (*Tōjin Okichi*, 1930, silent)
AND YET THEY GO (*Shikamo Karera wa Yuku*, 1931, silent)
THE MAN OF THE MOMENT (*Toki no Ujigami*, 1932, sound)
THE DAWN OF MANCHURIA AND MONGOLIA (*Manmō Kenkoku no Reimei*, 1932, sound)
*WHITE THREADS OF THE CASCADE (*Taki no Shiraito*) (Irie Production, 1933, silent)
Producer: Takako Irie
Screenplay: Yasunaga Higashibōjō, Shinji Masuda and Kennosuke Tateoka

Photography: Shigeru Miki
Cast: Takako Irie (Taki no Shiraito), Tokihiko Okada (Kinya Murakoshi)
Running Time: 110 minutes
Premiere: 1 June 1933
Rental: Not in distribution
GION FESTIVAL (*Gion Matsuri*, 1933, silent)
THE JINPŪ GROUP (*Jinpūren*, 1934, silent)

Sound Films
THE MOUNTAIN PASS OF LOVE AND HATE (*Aizō Tōge*, 1934)
*THE DOWNFALL OF OSEN (*Orizuru Osen*) (Daiichi Eiga, 1935)
Screenplay: Tatsunosuke Takashima
Photography: Minoru (or Shigeto) Miki
Cast: Isuzu Yamada (Osen), Daijirō Natsukawa (Sōkichi Hata)
Running Time: 78 minutes
Premiere: 20 January 1935
Rental: Not in distribution
*OYUKI THE MADONNA (*Maria no Oyuki*) (Daiichi Eiga, 1935)
Screenplay: Tatsunosuke Takashima
Photography: Minoru Miki
Sound: Junichi Murota
Cast: Isuzu Yamada (Oyuki), Komako Hara (Okin), Daijirō Natsukawa (Shingo
    Asakura)
Running Time: 78 minutes
Premiere: 30 May 1935
Rental: Not in distribution
*POPPY (*Gubijinsō*) (Daiichi Eiga, 1935)
Screenplay: Haruo Takayanagi
Photography: Minoru Miki
Cast: Daijirō Natsukawa (Hajime Munechika), Ichirō Tsukida (Seizō Ono),
    Chiyoko Ōkura (Sayoko Inoue), Kuniko Miyake (Fujio Kōno)
Running Time: 72 minutes
Premiere: 31 October 1935
Rental: Not in distribution
*OSAKA ELEGY (*Naniwa Erejī*) (Daiichi Eiga, 1936)
Screenplay: Yoshikata Yoda and Kenji Mizoguchi
Photography: Minoru Miki
Music: Kōichi Takagi
Cast: Isuzu Yamada (Ayako), Benkei Shiganoya (Asai), Yōko Umemura (Sumiko
    Asai), Eitarō Shindō (Fujino)
Running Time: 66 minutes
Premiere: 28 May 1936
Rental: Films Inc.
*SISTERS OF THE GION (*Gion no Shimai*) (Daiichi Eiga, 1936)
Screenplay: Yoshikata Yoda and Kenji Mizoguchi
Photography: Minoru Miki
Cast: Isuzu Yamada (Omocha), Yōko Umemura (Umekichi)

Running Time: 69 minutes
Premiere: 15 October 1936
Rental: Films, Inc.
*THE STRAITS OF LOVE AND HATE (*Aienkyō*) (Shinkō Kinema, 1937)
Screenplay: Yoshikata Yoda and Kenji Mizoguchi
Photography: Minoru Miki
Art Director: Hiroshi Mizutani
Cast: Fumiko Yamaji (Ofumi), Seizaburō Kawazu (Yoshitarō), Masao Shimizu (Kenkichi)
Running Time: 88 minutes
Premiere: 17 June 1937
Rental: Not in distribution
THE SONG OF THE CAMP (*Roei no Uta*, 1938)
AH, MY HOME TOWN (*Aa, Kokyō*, 1938)
*THE STORY OF THE LAST CHRYSANTHEMUM (*Zangiku Monogatari*) (Shōchiku Kyoto, 1939)
Screenplay: Yoshikata Yoda
Photography: Shigeto Miki
Art Director: Hiroshi Mizutani
Cast: Shōtarō Hanayagi (Kikunosuke Onoe), Kakuko Mori (Otoku)
Running Time: 142 minutes
Premiere: 13 October 1939
Rental: Films Inc.
THE WOMAN OF OSAKA (*Naniwa Onna*, 1940)
THE LIFE OF AN ACTOR (*Geidō Ichidai Otoko*, 1941)
*THE LOYAL 47 RONIN, parts 1-2 (*Genroku Chūshingura*, parts 1–2) (Shōchiku Kōa Eiga, 1941–42)
Screenplay: Kenichirō Hara and Yoshikata Yoda
Photography: Kōhei Sugiyama
Art Director: Hiroshi Mizutani and Kaneto Shindō
Cast: Chōjūrō Kawarazaki (Kuranosuke Ōishi), Yoshizaburō Arashi (Takuminokami Asano), Utaemon Ichikawa (Tsunatoyo Tokugawa), Mieko Takamine (Omino)
Running Time: 222 minutes
Premiere: 1 December 1941 (part 1); 11 February 1942 (part 2)
Rental: Films Inc.
THREE GENERATIONS OF DANJŪRO (*Danjūrō Sandai*, 1944)
*MUSASHI MIYAMOTO (*Miyamoto Musashi*) (Shōchiku Kyoto, 1944)
Screenplay: Matsutarō Kawaguchi
Photography: Shigeto Miki
Cast: Chōjūrō Kawarazaki (Musashi), Kinuyo Tanaka (Shinobu)
Running Time: 53 minutes
Premiere: 28 December 1944
Rental: Not in distribution
*THE FAMOUS SWORD BIJOMARU (*Meitō Bijomaru*) (Shochiku Kyōto, 1945)
Screenplay: Matsutarō Mawaguchi

Photography: Shigeto Miki and Haruo Takeno
Cast: Shōtarō Hanayagi (Kiyone Sakurai), Isuzu Yamada (Sasae Onoda)
Running Time: 65 minutes
Premiere: 8 February 1945
Rental: Not in distribution
VICTORY SONG (*Hisshōka*, 1945)
*THE VICTORY OF WOMEN (*Josei no Shōri*) (Shōchiku Ōfuna, 1946)
Screenplay: Kōgo Noda and Kaneto Shindō
Photography: Toshio Ubukata
Cast: Kinuyo Tanaka (Hiroko Hosokawa), Michiko Kuwano (Michiko), Mitsuko
    Miura (Moto Asakura), Shin Tokudaiji (Keita Yamaoka)
Running Time: 84 minutes
Premiere: 18 April 1946
Rental: Not in distribution
*UTAMARO AND HIS FIVE WOMEN (Utamaro o Meguru Gonin no Onna)
    (Shōchiku Kyoto, 1946)
Screenplay: Yoshikata Yoda
Photography: Shigeto Miki
Cast: Minosuke Bandō (Utamaro), Kinuyo Tanaka (Okita)
Running Time: 106 minutes
Premiere: 17 December 1946
Rental: New Yorker Films
*THE LOVE OF SUMAKO THE ACTRESS (*Joyū Sumako no Koi*) (Shōchiku
    Kyoto, 1947)
Screenplay: Yoshikata Yoda
Photography: Shigeto Miki
Cast: Kinuyo Tanaka (Sumako Matsui), Sō Yamamura (Hōgetsu Shimamura)
Running Time: 96 minutes
Premiere: 16 August 1947
Rental: Not in distribution.
*WOMEN OF THE NIGHT (*Yoru no Onnatachi*) (Shōchiku Kyoto, 1948)
Producer: Hisao Itoya
Screenplay: Yoshikata Yoda
Photography: Kōhei Sugiyama
Art Director: Hiroshi Mizutani
Cast: Kinuyo Tanaka (Fusako Ōwada), Sanae Takasugi (Natsuko Kimishima)
Running Time: 105 minutes
Premiere: 28 May 1948
Rental: Films Inc.
*MY LOVE HAS BEEN BURNING (*Waga Koi wa Moenu*) (Shōchiku Kyoto,
    1949)
Producer: Hisao Itoya
Screenplay: Yoshikata Yoda and Kaneto Shindō
Photography: Kōhei Sugiyama
Art Director: Hiroshi Mizutani
Cast: Kinuyo Tanaka (Eiko Hirayama), Ichirō Sugai (Kentarō Omoi), Mitsuko
    Mito (Chiyo)
Running Time: 96 minutes

Premiere: 13 February 1949
Rental: New Yorker Films
*A PICTURE OF MADAME YUKI (*Yuki Fujin Ezu*) (Shin Tōhō, 1950)
Producer: Kazuo Takimura
Screenplay: Yoshikata Yoda and Kazurō Funahashi
Art Director: Hiroshi Mizutani
Cast: Michiyo Kogure (Yuki Shinano), Yoshiko Kuga (Hamako Abe), Ken Uehara
(Masaya Kikunaka), Eijirō Yanagi (Naoyuki Shinano)
Running Time: 88 minutes
Premiere: 14 October 1950
Rental: Not in distribution
*MISS OYŪ (*Oyūsama*) (Daiei Kyoto, 1951)
Producer: Masaichi Nagata
Screenplay: Yoshikata Yoda
Photography: Kazuo Miyagawa
Art Director: Hiroshi Mizutani
Cast: Kinuyo Tanaka (Oyū), Nobuko Otowa (Oshizu), Yūji Hori (Shinnosuke)
Running Time: 96 minutes
Premiere: 22 June 1951
Rental: Not in distribution
*THE LADY OF MUSASHINO (*Musashino Fujin*) (Tōhō, 1951)
Producer: Hideo Koi
Screenplay: Yoshikata Yoda
Photography: Masao Tamai
Art Director: Takashi Matsuyama
Cast: Kinuyo Tanaka (Michiko Akiyama), Masayuki Mori (Tadao Akiyama),
Akihiko Katayama (Tsutomu Miyaji)
Running Time: 88 minutes
Premiere: 14 September 1951
Rental: Not in distribution
*THE LIFE OF OHARU (*Saikaku Ichidai Onna*) (Shin Tōhō, 1952)
Screenplay: Yoshikata Yoda
Photography: Yoshimi Hirano
Art Director: Hiroshi Mizutani
Cast: Kinuyo Tanaka (Oharu), Toshirō Mifune (Katsunosuke), Eitarō Shindō
(Kabei Sasaya), Sadako Sawamura (Owasa)
Running Time: 137 minutes
Premiere: 3 April 1952
Rental: New Yorker Films
*UGETSU (*Ugetsu Monogatari*) (Daiei Kyōto, 1953)
Producer: Masaichi Nagata
Screenplay: Yoshikata Yoda
Photography: Kazuo Miyagawa
Art Director: Kisaku Itō
Music: Fumio Hayasaka
Cast: Machiko Kyō (Wakasa), Masayuki Mori (Genjūrō), Kinuyo Tanaka
(Miyagi), Sakae Ozawa (Tōbei), Mitsuko Mito (Ohama)
Running Time: 97 minutes

Premiere: 26 March 1953
Rental: Films Inc; Budget Films: EmGee Film Library: The Images Films
  Archive, Inc; Kit Parker Films; V.C.I. Films; Bauer International
*GION FESTIVAL MUSIC (*Gion Bayashi*) (Daiei Kyoto, 1953)
Producer: Hisakazu Tsuji
Screenplay: Yoshikata Yoda
Photography: Kazuo Miyagawa
Art Director: Kazumi Koike
Cast: Michiyo Kogure (Miyoharu), Ayako Wakao (Eiko)
Running Time: 85 minutes
Premiere: 12 August 1953
Rental: New Yorker Films
*SANSHŌ THE BAILIFF (*Sanshō Dayū*) (Daiei Kyoto, 1954)
Producer: Masaichi Nagata
Screenplay: Fuji Yahiro and Yoshikata Yoda
Photography: Kazuo Miyagawa
Cast: Kinuyo Tanaka (Tamaki), Kishō Hanayagi (Zushiō), Kyōko Kagawa (Anju),
  Eitarō Shindō (Sanshō Dayū)
Running Time: 88 minutes
Premiere: 31 March 1954
Rental: Films Inc.
*THE WOMAN OF THE RUMOR (*Uwasa no Onna*) (Daiei Kyoto, 1954)
Screenplay: Yoshikata Yoda and Masashige Narusawa
Photography: Kazuo Miyagawa
Art Director: Hiroshi Mizutani
Music: Toshirō Mayuzumi
Cast: Kinuyo Tanaka (Hatsuko Umabuchi), Yoshiko Kuga (Yukiko Umabuchi),
  Tomoemon Ōtani (Kenji Matoba)
Running Time: 83 minutes
Premiere: 20 June 1954
Rental: Not in distribution
*THE CRUCIFIED LOVERS (*Chikamatsu Monogatari*) (Daiei Tokyo, 1954)
Producer: Masaichi Nagata
Screenplay: Yoshikata Yoda
Photography: Kazuo Miyagawa
Art Director: Hiroshi Mizutani
Music: Fumio Hayasaka
Cast: Kazuo Hasegawa (Mohei), Kyōko Kagawa (Osan)
Running Time: 102 minutes
Premiere: 23 November 1954
Rental: New Line Cinema
*THE PRINCESS YANG KWEI-FEI (*Yōkihi*) (Daiei Tokyo, 1955)
Producer: Masaichi Nagata and Run-run Shaw
Screenplay: T'ao Ch'in, Matsutarō Kawaguchi, Yoshikata Yoda and Masashige
  Narusawa
Photography: Kōhei Sugiyama (in color)
Art Director: Hiroshi Mizutani

Cast: Machiko Kyō (Yang Kwei-fei), Masayuki Mori (Emperor Hsuan-tsung), Sō
Yamamura (An Lu-shan)
Running Time: 98 minutes
Premiere: 3 May 1955
Rental: New Yorker Films
*NEW TALES OF THE TAIRA CLAN (*Shin Heike Monogatari*) (Daiei Kyoto,
1955)
Producer: Masaichi Nagata
Screenplay: Yoshikata Yoda, Masashige Narusawa, and Hisakazu Tsuji
Photography: Kazuo Miyagawa (in color)
Art Director: Hiroshi Mizutani
Cast: Raizō Ichikawa (Kiyomori), Yoshiko Kuga (Tokiko), Michiyo Kogure
(Yasuko), Ichijirō Ōya (Tadamori)
Running Time: 108 minutes
Premiere: 21 September 1955
Rental: New Line Cinema
*STREET OF SHAME (*Akasen Chitai*) (Daiei Kyoto, 1966)
Producer: Masaichi Nagata
Screenplay: Masashige Narusawa
Photography: Kazuo Miyagawa
Art Director: Hiroshi Mizutani
Music: Toshirō Mayuzumi
Cast: Machiko Kyō (Mickey), Ayako Wakao (Yasumi), Aiko Mimasu (Yumeko),
Michiyo Kogure (Hanae), Yasuko Kawakami (Shizuko)
Running Time: 94 minutes
Premiere: 18 March 1956
Rental: Films Inc.

Index

184